BLOOD ROYAL

Blood Royal

A Play in Three Acts

Elizabeth Jenkins

Edited, designed and produced by Tandem Publishing
http://tandempublishing.yolasite.com/

Cover illustration by Toby Ward.

ISBN: 979-8-39808-492-4

10 9 8 7 6 5 4 3 2 1

A CIP catalogue record for this book is available from the British Library.

Contents

CHARACTERS

KING CHARLES II

JAMES, DUKE OF YORK

JAMES FITZROY, DUKE OF MONMOUTH
The King's natural son

LORD SHAFTESBURY Lord Chancellor of England

LORD BRUCE A gentleman of the King's Bedchamber

LORD HALIFAX

LORD SUNDERLAND

MR CHIFFINCH Groom of the King's Closet

MR KNOLLYS	)	
MR BURGIN	)	
MR BUTTERFIELD	)	MPs
MR WEBSTER	)	

TITUS OATES A perjurer

MR PUMPHREY The King's clockmaker

4 CITIZENS OF OXFORD

3 MORE LORDS

CATHERINE OF BRAGANZA Wife to the King

LOUISE DE KÉROUALLE Duchess of Portsmouth

NELL GWYN

LADY ROBERTS Lady-in-Waiting to the Queen

DR KEN Bishop

ACT I

SCENE I The scene is a drawing-room in the King's suite in Whitehall. It is panelled in dark wood. At the left of the opposite wall is a door communicating with a gallery in the same wall, to the right a sash window. Between the door and window is a beautiful Chinese lacquer cabinet on a carved stand; on top of the cabinet is an ornate and beautiful clock of tortoiseshell and gold. In the right-hand wall is a marble fireplace with a moulded overmantel reaching to the ceiling; in the left, a door leading to a closet. On the walls are a van Dyke portrait of King Charles I, and a glowing vivid picture of some naked nymphs. By the hearth, facing the audience is an armchair covered in brocade patterned with tulips; in the centre of the stage, a small table with a drawer in it, containing writing materials; a carved chair with a cane seat is at the head of the table with its back to the fire. The room is lit by a huge sparkling chandelier, covered with garlands, stars and pendants of crystal.

(It is now mid-day; FOUR MEMBERS of Parliament are waiting to pay their respects to the KING; they have been waiting some time and are half-impatient, half-nervous. KNOLLYS is a plain country gentleman, BUTTERFIELD a would-be man of fashion, WEBSTER an honest Yorkshire squire, and BURGIN a crabby old man discontented with the present regime.)

BUTTERFIELD   What time is it now?

KNOLLYS   (Examining the clock) Quarter to twelve.

BUTTERFIELD   I suppose His Majesty is very busy.

BURGIN   Eh?

BUTTERFIELD   His Majesty's busy.

[3]

BURGIN   (In the loud voice of the deaf) Busy! Well, I take it there is no harm in my sitting down. (He stumps over to the big chair)

BUTTERFIELD   I suppose not, though it's not what I should do myself.

BURGIN   (Banging his stick between his knees) Young man! I have sat down in the presence of Oliver Cromwell.

BUTTERFIELD   (Superciliously) Perhaps so, sir, but that, fortunately, is of no consequence now.

BURGIN   Of no consequence now, sir! Let me tell you, sir —

BUTTERFIELD   And pray, sir, since you are on the topic, allow me to tell you.

KNOLLYS   Gentlemen, pray, for God's sake remember where you are!

BUTTERFIELD   Yes, indeed. His Majesty will think there is no notion of breeding in the country.

BURGIN   He hasn't got his ear to the door, has he?

BUTTERFIELD   He may come in at any moment —

BURGIN   Let 'un. Let 'un. That's what we are here for, isn't it?

BUTTERFIELD   (Turning his back) Really, Mr Knollys, it is extremely painful to be obliged to pay one's addresses to His Majesty in such company! We shall all be taken for a pack of yokels.

KNOLLYS   Don't be uneasy, Mr Butterfield, His Majesty is extremely pleasant and affable, and you know the ceremonial is not what it was in His late Majesty's time.

WEBSTER   Well, it's ceremonial enough for me! Such a

bowing and scraping and 'This way, gentlemen!' 'By your leave gentlemen!' It makes my head go round.

(CHIFFINCH, the KING's valet, a small, neat man, enters from the closet door, L.)

CHIFFINCH   Gentlemen, Lord Bruce, His Majesty's Gentleman of the Bedchamber, will be with you in a moment. He can tell you when to expect His Majesty. Won't you be seated, gentlemen?

BURGIN   There! What did I say? (Chuckles)

WEBSTER   (Coming forward) And who be ye, lad?

CHIFFINCH   (Pertly) Mr Chiffinch, Groom of the Closet, at your service, sir.

(Exit)

BURGIN   (Groaning) Ah! I have heard of that Chiffinch. A son of Belial. Groom of the Closet, indeed! A Groom of the Backstairs, more like!

BUTTERFIELD   (In desperation) For God's sake, Mr Burgin! You will be taken for I don't know what!

BURGIN   As long as they don't take me for a bloody Papist, let them take me as they find me.

BUTTERFIELD   Really, sir, I must ask)
you —)
)
WEBSTER   Hear! Hear! My sentiment!)   (Together)
)
KNOLLYS   I beg that you'll remember)
where we are, sir.)

(CHIFFINCH opens the closet door, and LORD BRUCE enters. He is a young man with an ingenuous,

trustworthy face. His manner is naturally civil
and kindly. He adores the KING and his love for
CHARLES colours almost everything he says and
supplies the key to it.)

CHIFFINCH   Lord Bruce, gentlemen.

(Exit)

BRUCE   Your servant, gentlemen. His Majesty and the Duke
of York are in the palace now. His Majesty desired me to say he
would be with you immediately. If you will do me the favour, I
had better know your names, and then I can present you singly.
(He consults a small note) Mr Knollys?

KNOLLYS   Here, sir!

BRUCE   Thank you. Mr Butterfield.

BUTTERFIELD   Your servant, sir.

BRUCE   Thank you. Mr Burgin?

(No answer)

WEBSTER   (Loudly) Mr Burgin!!

BURGIN   Eh! Oh! Here! Here!

BRUCE   And Mr Webster?

WEBSTER   Here, my lord.

BRUCE   Thank you.

WEBSTER   (Coming forward and speaking with hesitation,
but solidly) My lord!

BRUCE   Sir?

WEBSTER   If so be as there is no offence taken where none is
meant…

BRUCE   (Civilly) None at all, sir.

WEBSTER   Could you tell us whether it is true or not that the Duke of York is really and truly a Papist?

BRUCE   Certainly, sir. It has never been denied that I know of; did you not hear of His Royal Highness being obliged by Parliament to resign his position in the Admiralty on account of his religion? His Royal Highness has been made to suffer so much for it, I am surprised anyone shouldn't know that he is a Catholic.

BUTTERFIELD   My lord, Mr Webster comes from a remote and barbarous region up in Yorkshire. Naturally he doesn't hear the half of what goes on.

BURGIN   (Growling) None the worse for that.

WEBSTER   Aye, but I like to know how things are; but there's another thing, my lord, though maybe I do wrong to speak of it…

BRUCE   It shall go no further, sir.

WEBSTER   You understand I mean no disrespect to His Majesty, God bless him! And it would be a poor thing if I did, since my father lost the best part of fifteen hundred pound, and twenty of the best horses as anybody ever saw, as well as melting down the salt cellars and the spoons, all to help King Charles I.

BRUCE   I am certain that His Majesty has no truer subject, Mr Webster, and if I can answer your question I will, as I am a gentleman.

WEBSTER   Thank 'ee, lad; it's this then. (Comes closer to BRUCE and emphasises his points with his fist on the palm of his other hand) The King and the Duke of York are brothers, ain't they?

BRUCE   Certainly, sir.

WEBSTER   Well, that 'ere Duke of Monmouth that everybody is so fond on, and is now fighting the Scots rebels, more power to his arm, is said by some, as is perhaps in the know, to be the Duke of York's nephew: but not the King's nephew. Now! What do 'ee make of that?

BRUCE (Half laughing) Why really, Mr Webster, the question is most discreetly put upon my honour. I don't know that anybody could have put it better if they had lived at court all their lives but one moment, gentlemen … my Lord Shaftesbury!

> (At this moment the door leading from the gallery has quietly opened and LORD SHAFTESBURY stands smiling on the threshold. His appearance, for all his amiability, is sinister in the extreme. His face has a livid pallor; he suffers from an ulcer in his side, which makes him move cautiously and he occasionally (but not in this scene) puts his hand to his side in pain. He is obviously a man of remarkable intellect; everybody on the stage appears childish by contrast)

SHAFTESBURY   Your servant, my lord. Who are these gentlemen?

BRUCE   Mr Knollys, Mr Butterfield, Mr Burgin, Mr Webster: come to pay their respects to His Majesty on their election to Parliament. Gentlemen, the Lord Chancellor my Lord Shaftesbury.

> (The SQUIRES all duck; BRUCE, who knows the KING's arch-enemy when he sees him, is as alert and restless as a faithful terrier. He knows that SHAFTESBURY has no business in the KING's rooms at this hour and has come to work mischief.)

(Bowing) I hope, my lord, there has been no mistake, your lordship's time is so valuable. Has not your lordship an appointment with His Majesty this evening?

SHAFTESBURY   (Amiably) If there is a mistake, Lord Bruce, I have made it; this poor head of mine! I had quite fancied my appointment with His Majesty was for twelve o'clock. However, I cannot regret it, since it gives me the opportunity of being personally known to these gentlemen. (Bowing to them. The SQUIRES look amazed under SHAFTESBURY's glib flow of talk)

(BRUCE stations himself extreme left, out of the picture but watching it)

Gentlemen, I am most happy; I must congratulate you on the position to which your discerning neighbours have elected you. To be a Member of Parliament in these times, gentlemen, is a heavy responsibility.

BRUCE   (Quietly) Why in these times especially, my lord?

SHAFTESBURY   My interesting friend Lord Bruce is, as you see, gentlemen, very young. Ah, youth! Youth! Carefree, thoughtless, the age of gold! But you, gentlemen, as the representatives of the nation, and I as its Chancellor, must address ourselves to the cares of state. Believe me, they will occupy us long and seriously. There are grave problems before the nation which, gentlemen, you come to help us solve. Economy and vigilance must be our watchwords.

WEBSTER   Ah!

SHAFTESBURY   Retrenchments must be made.

WEBSTER   Ah!

SHAFTESBURY   Supplies apportioned to the purpose for which they are voted; and more than this, gentlemen. The present is not our only care. The future of the realm, the succession of the crown is also before us: fearful perils must be scanned afar off and prepared for ere they come upon us; in one word, gentlemen, patriotism!

WEBSTER   (Seizing upon the one point he has been able to understand) Aye, we do hear there's a powerful lot of money spent.

BURGIN   Speaking of perils, my lord, I beg to say that the worst peril that could overtake this country would be a return to the Church of Rome. We've seen something of the Papists' handiwork in the Great Fire.

BUTTERFIELD   Come, sir, that's going too far.

KNOLLYS   I don't think that's been proved, sir.

BURGIN   Don't tell me, sir. I know better. Fine gentlemen can say what they like; but ask the honest townsfolk of England to say who are their enemies.

KNOLLYS   Really, Mr Burgin: I am an elected member as well as you; and my constituents would not go so far in abusing their neighbours who happened to be Catholics.

BURGIN   (In a passion) Then, sir, your constituents are fools and jackasses, and the sons of darkness. We know who are preparing to burn down our houses, ravish our wives and daughters, and spit our infants upon pikes. And I say again, sir, that a return to the Church of Rome would be the destruction and casting away of every honest man and woman in the kingdom.

KNOLLYS   (Apologetically to SHAFTESBURY) Mr Burgin is warm, your lordship.

SHAFTESBURY   I am delighted to find such a supporter of our national liberties.

BURGIN   And the best champion we ever had against the Pope, I don't care where I say it or who hears me say it, was Oliver Cromwell. God rest his bones!

> (This is a little too outspoken for SHAFTESBURY, who answers with the ghost of a furtive look at the others)

SHAFTESBURY   Your zeal, sir, is that of an honest man, but I assure you, there are champions of the present day, His Majesty…

BURGIN   Saving your lordship's presence, we hear a great deal too much about tolerance in these days. Tolerance! It cuts both ways, for Papists as well as Puritans. It's a damned sight better to have no toleration for anybody than to have it for the wrong people!

SHAFTESBURY   (Delighted) A Daniel come to judgement. Positively, sir, it warms my heart to hear you.

BRUCE   (Trembling with indignation) To warm your heart, my lord, it would be worthwhile listening even to treason!

SHAFTESBURY   (Stopping short, with a most kindly air) Treason! Treason! Who is talking of treason? My lord, your delightfully enthusiastic way of talking does me good, it does indeed, but you must be careful. Such an ugly word! Hanged, drawn and quartered! Shocking, quite shocking. Promise me, for your own sake, for sake of your friends, to be a little more guarded in your expressions!

BRUCE   (Vanquished) I humbly beg your lordship's pardon if I said anything amiss.

SHAFTESBURY   (Carelessly) Nothing, nothing whatever. Well, gentlemen, we are devoted, consecrated may I not say, to a sacred task: the service of our country; and believe me when I say that I rejoice that I shall have the assistance and support of men such as you in the critical times before us. For I will not disguise from you that I foresee a grave danger to us, and that is —

(Behind SHAFTESBURY'S back, CHIFFINCH opens the door from the gallery and announces, at the end of the last sentence —)

CHIFFINCH   His Royal Highness the Duke of York.

(Exit)

(YORK comes in, a tall, awkward man dressed in a crude shade of blue. He shows none of the Stuart grace and charm, but he has a certain dignity of his own and though it can be seen at a glance that he is a stupid man, his honesty is also patent, and this, together with the evidence of suffering and melancholy, gives him a kind of interest. At his entry, SHAFTESBURY sinks into the background and becomes one of the circle.)

YORK   (Languidly) Good morning, my lord.

BRUCE   Good morning, Your Royal Highness.

YORK   His Majesty is not here, I perceive.

BRUCE   We expect the King at any moment, sir.

SHAFTESBURY   No doubt His Majesty has been detained by some affair of importance, Your Royal Highness, I am sure it will do the loyal hearts of these gentlemen good to see how utterly devoted His Majesty is to the cares of state: ceaseless toil, unremitting application, the most unstinting sacrifice of self...

(CHIFFINCH opens the gallery door again and comes up to BRUCE)

CHIFFINCH   His Majesty has entered the gallery, my lord.

(Exit through the closet door)

BRUCE   Gentlemen, His Majesty.

(There is a pause of a few seconds as everyone faces the door expectantly. In a moment CHARLES appears; he is tall, extremely graceful, with a sallow, ugly but most attractive face; his periwig is black. He wears a grey coat, a waistcoat embroidered with crimson rosebuds, beautiful lace, and silver shoe buckles. His whole appearance exhibits the exquisite taste which is one of the characteristics of his unfortunate family. At his entrance everyone bows)

CHARLES   (Gaily and graciously) Good morning, my lords and gentlemen. I beg you'll forgive my causing you to wait. I've been playing tennis.

(SHAFTESBURY looks at the SQUIRES to see how they take this)

Good morning, brother. My Lord Shaftesbury, I was not expecting the pleasure of a visit from you till after dinner. However I am at your disposal if the matter is urgent.

(SHAFTESBURY is about to speak, but CHARLES turns to the SQUIRES)

Gentlemen, I am very much obliged to you all for coming to see me.

(BRUCE presents them)

BRUCE   Mr Knollys, Mr Butterfield, Mr Burgin, Mr Webster, sir. All new members of Your Majesty's Parliament.

(They kiss his hand in turn)

SHAFTESBURY   May I hope Your Majesty has enjoyed your game?

CHARLES   (With an accent of peevishness) Ah, I can't get anyone to <u>play with me</u>.

YORK   (Aroused at the idea that the representative of the Stuart family should not be gratified in every particular) Surely, sir, any of your gentlemen would be honoured…

CHARLES   (With an un-English shrug) They're honoured, but they can't play. I give them thirty points and beat them at the finish. No one can give me a game now the Duke of Monmouth is away.

BRUCE   But Your Majesty beats the Duke of Monmouth.

CHARLES   I do, but only just, Bruce. Jamie is a good tennis player, but the rogue can't get the better of his father! (Pause)

> (CHARLES laughs. SHAFTESBURY watches acutely. BURGIN and WEBSTER catch each other's eye, one in an expression of gratified disgust, the latter with open-mouthed astonishment.)

(Who has also been watching) Mr Webster, you and I have met before.

WEBSTER   Your Majesty! You can't remember that? It's not possible!

CHARLES   In Warwickshire.

WEBSTER   On Edgehill.

CHARLES   One evening.

WEBSTER   In the camp…

CHARLES   You brought me a pony from your father's estate.

WEBSTER   I did, Your Majesty! To think of your remembering! What a head Your Majesty has, to be sure! You were such a bonnie little lad, with eyes as black as sloes!

CHARLES   Was I! The pony was a gallant creature, with an undipped coat. I lost him when I was sent into the west.

WEBSTER   Twelve years old Your Majesty was at the time. We brought the horses for His Majesty your father, and my father said, 'Maybe the Prince, as is but a lad, would like one of the ponies.'

CHARLES   I did like him, Mr Webster, very much. I remember that evening as if it were yesterday. Sunset, was it not, a dark sky and a strip of light running round the edges of the fields?

WEBSTER   Yes, sir. We were brought into the middle of the tents, just where the Royal Standard was pitched; and there His Majesty was standing. It was the first time I ever set eyes on him: and the last.

CHARLES   (Pointing to the portrait) That picture, Mr Webster, do you think it a likeness?

WEBSTER   Wonderful, wonderful likeness, but His Majesty was a pleasanter-looking gentleman than that, all the same.

(CHARLES laughs. SHAFTESBURY takes a step forward as if to study the picture respectfully. The

others stare. YORK has been touched by the personal
loyalty of WEBSTER and speaks to him)

YORK   We consider that a very happy likeness, Mr Webster,
there is something in the dignity and reserve that exactly recalls
His late Majesty.

WEBSTER   (Who is shy at once with YORK, bowing) May
be, sir.

CHARLES   But you forget, brother. Mr Webster's only
memory of our father was when he came before him to receive
the thanks due to a loyal servant. There was a smile for Mr
Webster which van Dyke has not caught, and I agree with Mr
Webster that the picture's the poorer for it.

YORK   With all due respect to His Majesty's taste, I will
tell you, Mr Webster, that that portrait recalls to me exactly
the glorious martyr my father, as I saw him in the last solemn
moments of his existence.

(WEBSTER looks appalled. The pleasantness of the
scene is frozen up immediately)

The last time that the assassins permitted him to see his children,
he said to me that the rebels might try, in the absence of my
brother, to make one of us younger ones a puppet in their foul
designs, and he charged me that I must never allow myself to
be made King while my brother lived. I replied: 'I will be torn
in pieces first.' I was nine years old at the time, and I have
been told that my reply struck the bystanders as something
remarkable.

SHAFTESBURY   A singular instance of sagacity and spirit in
so young a child, Your Highness.

(The KING sees that his brother is being made a fool of)

CHARLES   Brother, are you riding today?

YORK   No, sire. If Your Majesty will excuse me, I intend to visit the stables.

CHARLES   If I were you I should go at once, and make the most of the morning. Shall you be long?

YORK   Why no, sire. The fact is, I have a small scheme of entertainment for this evening; I want to ask the favour of the Duchess of Portsmouth's presence at it, before I go. Lady Chesterfield has discovered a boy with an angelic voice; the plan was to have a little impromptu concert: nothing tedious, you understand; and a small supper afterwards.

CHARLES   I am sure the Duchess will be delighted. Good day, brother, and I hope you will find the hunters doing well.

(YORK makes his exit)

(CHARLES sees that BURGIN is the hostile member of the party and addresses him)

Mr Burgin, how goes the glove trade today? I believe that is what your region of Warwickshire is principally noted for?

BURGIN   Well enough, Your Majesty, so long as we get no interference from the French.

CHARLES   If the good wishes of a man with a pair of French gloves on his hands mayn't be deemed an insult, I wish the industry well with all my heart. But indeed, Mr Burgin, these you see were a present; you may be sure that when I buy, Warwickshire shall furnish me.

BURGIN   All the better for us, sir.

CHARLES   At the same time, Mr Burgin, have you ever considered that if we have no imports, we lose the import duties?

WEBSTER   Aye, so! That's true enough,   )
Mr Burgin!   )   (Together)

BUTTERFIELD   Your Majesty is right.   )

KNOLLYS   Ah! There's the point!   )

CHARLES   You gentlemen in Parliament are not very liberal you know, yet I must maintain the navy and pay the few soldiers I keep. If we were invaded and found unprepared, something tells me, Mr Burgin, that your voice would not be silent among the uproar?

BURGIN   (Working up for an oration) I hope, sir, I know when to speak and when to hold my tongue, and I beg leave…

CHARLES   I have no doubt you do, sir, and what a blessing that is! Tedious conversation is the curse of the age, is it not? How happy those are who never offend in this way, nor suffer themselves to be offended! (To SHAFTESBURY) My lord, I know you have business with me, no matter for the time; if these gentlemen will excuse us, we will proceed to it.

CHIFFINCH   (Entering from the closet and approaching the KING) May it please Your Majesty, Her Grace the Duchess of Portsmouth begs to know if Your Majesty will see her for a few moments.

SHAFTESBURY   (Bowing) Your Majesty, my business is of no immediate importance, I entreat that it may not stand in the way of other – more agreeable – matters.

CHARLES   (To CHIFFINCH) Tell the Duchess that I await

her here. Gentlemen, you will not leave the palace without taking some refreshment, I hope. Chiffinch, conduct these gentlemen to the second table. I wish you good morning, gentlemen.

BRUCE   (Advancing) If you will follow Mr Chiffinch, gentlemen, he will see you are attended to.

CHARLES   Bruce, I will see Her Grace, the Duchess of Portsmouth, now.

(Exit BRUCE R.)

(The SQUIRES take leave of SHAFTESBURY and BRUCE and prepare to follow CHIFFINCH from the room into the gallery. At the door, WEBSTER turns to the KING)

WEBSTER   I can't get over your remembering that pony, Your Majesty!

(Exeunt SQUIRES & CHIFFINCH)

SHAFTESBURY   (Smiling) Your Majesty, I will retire and present myself again this evening. (He appears to be winning and confidential) I trust that it will be convenient to Your Majesty to see me then, I am most unwilling to be tedious, but it is really important that I…

CHARLES   As I have made the appointment, my lord, I daresay I will keep it.

SHAFTESBURY   I thank Your Majesty. (He goes towards the gallery door)

(Exit SHAFTESBURY)

BRUCE   Her Grace the Duchess of Portsmouth, Your Majesty.

(The DUCHESS enters L. She is extremely beautiful: young, with black curling hair, and her complexion set off by the deep mourning that she wears. She has an almost infantile vacuousness of expression, yet it is clear that this is the mask over a heartless and mercenary character. Similarly, though her attitudes are exquisitely graceful, they are all studied; she would never make a spontaneous gesture except in anger or fright. CHARLES's passion is obvious: as is also the fact that he has never had, and never will have, a kiss or a favour without paying heavily for it.)

(BRUCE exits)

LOUISE   Your Majesty is very kind to grant me this interview.

CHARLES   (Protesting) My dear! It is I who am the obliged person.

(He kisses her hand. She throws herself gracefully into a chair)

LOUISE   Ah! You are always so gracious.

CHARLES   It is you, ma cherie, who are gracious.

LOUISE   Alas! I must blush when I hear you or anyone else say so.

CHARLES   Why, my dear, aren't you used to it by now?

LOUISE   Sire, if I thought myself in danger of losing my self-respect, I would relinquish your court without a sigh and return to the humble but peaceful solitude of my home in Brittany.

CHARLES   Oddsfish, my dear! Don't talk like that.

LOUISE   (Perceiving the effect she has made) Indeed, I often ponder upon the manner of my return there.

CHARLES   But, Louise, is anything here wanting to your comfort? Can I do anything for you?

LOUISE   (Sharply) I positively require some money, sir.

CHARLES   (Blankly) Oh!

LOUISE   If it were not a necessity, I would not speak of it.

CHARLES   Has not the treasurer paid your quarter's income?

LOUISE   It is entirely inadequate, sir.

CHARLES   (Distressed) I'm sorry; I know that I don't maintain you as you deserve; but I give you as much as I have.

LOUISE   I should never recover from it, sir, if I thought I appeared to you in the least degree mercenary.

CHARLES   Not in the least, my life.

LOUISE   But there are certain elegancies without which, to a person of my birth, existence is insupportable.

CHARLES   What is it you must have, my dear? You know I find it very difficult at present to pay my household's salaries.

LOUISE   It is a diamond necklace, sir. It has been on view at the Goldsmiths' Company for the past month. Everyone has seen it; and several people have been kind enough to say that there is only one person in the kingdom who could properly wear it. (She preens herself) And of course, as day after day goes by without its being bought, everybody talks: and it's very mortifying to me.

CHARLES   How much does it cost?

LOUISE   Twenty thousand pounds.

CHARLES   Good God!

LOUISE   But they would let you pay ten thousand down and interest on the rest until it was convenient.

CHARLES   The devil they would!

LOUISE   If you are so short of money, surely there is some way in which you could retrench?

CHARLES   (Dryly) Oh! Undoubtedly!

LOUISE   Then surely —

CHARLES   Well, my love, I will see what can be done. If I must buy this damned necklace, it will be some consolation to see it round the most beautiful neck in the world. (He kisses her) But you're in mourning, my Louise? For whom is it this time?

(The DUCHESS speaks in a silvery voice, with an air of surprise)

LOUISE   Has Your Majesty not heard of the death of the Chevalier de Rohan? The distressing news arrived this morning.

CHARLES   Certainly I had heard of it, but I didn't know you were related to him?

LOUISE   O, but closely! I could not possibly avoid the compliment of deep mourning.

CHARLES   My dear Louise, considering the rate at which your relations die off, what a blessing it is that black is so becoming to you.

LOUISE   Ah, now Your Majesty is making game of me. Alas! I cannot help my exalted birth!

CHARLES   But at least I hope that however closely related you and the Chevalier may have been, you don't suffer personally at his death? (Tenderly) For, indeed, Louise, I should be very sorry to see you in grief, not only because I am a happy, grateful lover; but because you came to me through my sister.

> (CHARLES's demeanour has become profoundly melancholy at the mention of his sister. The DUCHESS feels obliged to make her contribution)

LOUISE   Ah, sir, the death of madame has put the whole of France into mourning.   (Pause)

What sadness you have had in your family life, mon pauvre Charles! To lose the two people you loved best, your sister and the King your father.

CHARLES   My father! Yes. I understand now that if he had lived till I was a grown man, we should have disagreed over a great many things; but then, I only knew him as the kindest father a boy ever had.

LOUISE   (Sweetly) Of course I was not born at the time. His murder must have been extremely shocking.

CHARLES   (Starting up) O God, why do I speak of it! I sent them a blank paper with my signature at the bottom for them to write any terms they pleased if only they would spare his life.

LOUISE   And what did they do?

CHARLES   Cromwell tore it up with his own hands.

LOUISE   Indeed, Charles, I wonder at the patience you showed when you came back. To execute the actual murderers only! And they say you wouldn't even be present at the executions!

CHARLES   I don't like punishing people; I think it has something to do with my not being a good man.

LOUISE   (Who has no sense of humour) Very probably; if you would declare yourself a good Catholic, the Church would show you whom you ought to punish; then it would not be your doing.

CHARLES   I daresay; but who said that we should forgive our enemies till seventy times seven?

LOUISE   But surely, Charles, you must realise – there is moderation in everything? Besides, I do not think it is right to talk like that.

CHARLES   (Humouring her) No, my dear. But you know what I am?

> (The DUCHESS rises from her chair and comes and puts her hands on his shoulders)

LOUISE   (Sweetly) But, Charles! I am sure that the true faith, the faith of the Queen, your mother, of the martyred Queen of Scots, your great-grandmother, of all those great kings and queens, has a place in your heart, has it not?

CHARLES   I won't deny it.

> (He is about to embrace her, but at his words she starts away and speaks with harsh fanaticism)

LOUISE   Then why don't you crush the Puritans? Those heretics, those blasphemers!

CHARLES   (With a shrug) I am not religious enough. It takes a champion of the Faith like His Majesty the King of France to have peasants slaughtered just because they are Protestants.

LOUISE   (Proudly) His Majesty the King of France is absolute in his dominions. Ah, what a hero! A model to the Kings of Christendom!

CHARLES   (Quietly) I will be absolute too.

LOUISE   (Admiring) That is my Charles!

CHARLES   And I don't care how deep I dig into the pockets of your master to make myself so —

LOUISE   (Eagerly) His Majesty will be only too happy to provide the necessary assistance.

CHARLES   And do you know for what reason I will achieve this?

LOUISE   (Surprised) Surely, to be absolute is an end in itself?

CHARLES   (In one of his rare moments of complete seriousness) I will be strong enough to let everybody go about his own business.

LOUISE   What an eccentric ideal.

CHARLES   (Taking her by the chin) Yes, you think power consists in stopping people from doing what they like. I want Puritans and Catholics to live side by side, each under his own vine and fig tree. You don't understand that, do you?

LOUISE   I must say, sir, since you ask me, I do not. And if you will pardon my saying so, I believe that if the King of France understood once and for all that you were so lax in your views about the Faith, His Majesty might scarcely be willing to … to … (She hesitates delicately)

CHARLES   (Bluntly) To come down with enough money to keep me independent of my Puritan Parliament. He doesn't do that as it is, but he'll have to, and for reasons quite unconnected with the state of my soul.

LOUISE   If Your Majesty will be good enough to explain?

CHARLES You've never seen my nephew, William, the Prince of Orange, have you?

LOUISE I have never had the honour of being presented to His Royal Highness.

CHARLES He is my sister Mary's son; some years ago I married him to my brother James's daughter. Poor girl! But I considered it absolutely necessary at the time. William is not lacking in spirit as you know, he turned your master's army out of Holland by opening the dykes, and flooding the land.

LOUISE (Nettled) I am aware of that.

CHARLES Er – precisely. Well, I can only hope she's found some way of amusing herself since; but the Dutch court is quite an English family party!

LOUISE I am sure that it is extremely charming.

CHARLES Damned dull. However, the English, as you know, and I confess it with shame, entertain this boorish prejudice against the French; unquestionably the politest nation on the face of the earth; and they would far rather see me allied to my nephew and the Dutch cheese and butter interest, than dignified by an alliance with His Majesty King Louis the Fourteenth.

LOUISE Yes, sir. And what guarantee has His Majesty that you will not, in spite of everything, yield to the wishes of your people, and form an alliance against him with the States of Holland!

CHARLES The best and only guarantee: self-interest. (He leans forward and speaks in a low, clear voice) Dutch trade can only flourish at the expense of English trade. The commerce of the world lies between Dutch ships and English ships. I don't want an army – to fight other people's battles for them at my expense. I want a navy. The English people don't realise the extent of their possibilities at sea, but they will, please God, before I've done with them. My ambition is trade, and the only people who can take it from me are the Dutch; and the only people who can give the Dutch something else to think about are the French. Let your master keep his word with me, and he needn't be afraid of my not keeping mine with him.

LOUISE   His Majesty has had such vast expenses of late: I am afraid he may require some other concession before he undertakes any substantial payment.

CHARLES   (Gallantly) That will be for you to argue. (Kissing her hand) So lovely an ambassadress cannot fail to bring us into agreement.

> (The DUCHESS throws herself back in her chair with an air of weakness)

LOUISE   Really, sir, if you send me over to France, I can't answer for it that I shall come back.

> (CHARLES gets up and stands over her)

CHARLES   Louise! Is my court no longer pleasant to you?

LOUISE   Of course I am devoted to Your Majesty. Alas! Have I not given the final proof of it?

CHARLES   I can ask nothing further, except a continuance of my good fortune.

LOUISE   Naturally, a parting would pain me very much, but I am being drawn to consider it.

CHARLES   (Peevish) O! You want to get something else out of me. You couldn't have thought of a better way. Tell me now, what is it you want?

LOUISE   The English are so gross – such savage monsters! To dare to revile me because I am a Catholic, and to say I spend too much money —

CHARLES   My love, I protect you in every way I can: for the rest, you have to take the English as you find them.

LOUISE   (Working herself into a passion) Never shall I forget that creature, Lady Montagu —

CHARLES   My dear, that is all over now!

LOUISE   (Disregarding him) To take my lodgings from under my nose.

CHARLES   Yes, yes...

LOUISE   (Screaming) And to say that titles purchased with prostitution commanded no respect from persons of quality and sense!

CHARLES   (Embracing her and leading her back to her chair) Did I not order out a troop of household cavalry to escort you back to my arms?

LOUISE   (Weakly) You were very kind, but you cannot understand these mortifications to a personage of my delicacy.

CHARLES   O my dear Louise, the weather has made you low-spirited; what a pity you are in mourning! We might have gone to the play this evening.

LOUISE   The theatre is very well in its way, but for a modest creature like myself it is spoilt by the impudence of the actresses —

> (A knocking is heard on the window and somebody is seen to be outside)

CHARLES   (Angrily) What's that?

(He goes to the window, gives an exclamation, and pulls up the sash. NELL GWYN is seen, apparently hoisted up to the level of the sill. CHARLES takes her in his arms and lifts her into the room. She is the greatest contrast to the Duchess. Her youth and health would make her fascinating even if she were not lovely, but she is, with nut-brown curling hair, and the true English colouring. She wears a bright rose-coloured dress and large pearl earrings and necklace, and has a very broad black scarf tied over one shoulder and under the other.)

(With unconcealed delight) Nelly, Nelly, how dare you intrude into the presence of your sovereign?

NELL   (Calling out of the window) Thank you, my lord. It's all right! (To CHARLES) It wasn't Lord Bruce's fault! I stood on his back. He didn't want me to. (She hugs the KING) You aren't angry, are you?

CHARLES   Well, no, but —

NELL   I had to fly to you! I need your sympathy!

CHARLES   (Trying not to laugh) What for?

NELL   (Pulling out her handkerchief) I am bereaved! Don't you see I am in mourning?

CHARLES   (Passing his hand over his mouth) For whom?

NELL   (Triumphantly) For the Cham of Tartary!

CHARLES   But what relation is the Cham of Tartary to you?

NELL   (Triumphantly) Exactly the same relation as the Chevalier de Rohan is to the Duchess of Portsmouth!

[29]

(She waits a second till CHARLES begins to laugh,
then joins him in a hearty roar. The DUCHESS looks
furious. CHARLES pulls himself together reluctantly.)

CHARLES   Very good. But take it off now, my dear
(Coaxingly) to please me.

NELL   O Charles! (Philosophically) Well, it's not the first time
I've undressed myself to please you...

CHARLES   Nor the last, I hope, Nelly.

(He helps her to unknot the scarf and fold it over her
arm; then he turns her towards the DUCHESS)

(Suggestively) You have not seen Her Grace the Duchess of
Portsmouth today, have you?

NELL   (Giving a slight curtsey) Always pleased to meet any
friend of yours, Charlie.

(The DUCHESS takes a few steps down the centre of
the room)

LOUISE   (Closing her eyes as if in great pain) Charlie! Is it
possible, madame, that you conceive yourself to be addressing
His Majesty King Charles the Second!

NELL   Charles the Second! Well, he's my Charles the Third!
(Counting on her fingers) There was Charles Saville and Charles
Hart, and —

LOUISE   Pray, madame, spare us the recital of your amours, to
give them no grosser name —

CHARLES   (Who has sat down and is watching her, lazily and
happily) Which Charles did you like best, Nelly?

NELL   (Frankly) I like Charles Stuart best; but I <u>did</u> like the others too, I'm not like the Duchess of Portsmouth who can love nobody but Kings!

LOUISE   (Sweetly) For a person of your station in life, madame, it would be exceedingly ridiculous and inconvenient for you if you were!

NELL   I don't know about station! I may be a Duchess one day!

LOUISE   His Majesty may make a Duchess; but even His Majesty cannot make a gentlewoman.

CHARLES   Now! Now! Tch! Tch! Tch!

NELL   (Ingenuously) I was born to be a doxy, but you're so fine and grand, I should have thought you'd never have consented to it.

LOUISE   (Aghast) Are you inferring, madame, any similarity between your condition and mine?

NELL   Certainly not. I'm popular! Did you hear, Charles, how my coach was held up by a rabble yesterday at Temple Bar?

CHARLES   No, what happened?

NELL   (Carelessly) O they shouted, and threw stones and dirt.

CHARLES   (Tenderly and shrewdly) You weren't frightened, Nelly?

NELL   Not at all, I knew they thought it was the Duchess of Portsmouth. I put my head out of the window and shouted out as loud as I could: Gently, good friends! I'm the Protestant whore!

> (The DUCHESS starts to her feet, trembling with rage, and speaks in a voice choked with fury)

LOUISE   I will return to France!

    (CHARLES is about to say something, but NELL interrupts)

NELL   O no you won't, my dear, not as long as the pickings here are so good. You won't make sixty thousand pounds a year in France!

CHARLES   Nelly, Nelly, that's ungenerous.

NELL   I'm sorry, Charlie.

CHARLES   It is to the Duchess you should apologise. Lady Portsmouth, you will overlook a little rudeness from a lady whose experience of court life is something less than your own!

    (The DUCHESS remembers that she is expected by the King of France to stay in England: and also that her consequence as CHARLES's mistress is very much greater than it would be in any other capacity. Needless to say, she has no intention whatever of leaving the country. She masters her rage and falls back on an exaggeration of her usual elegance.)

LOUISE   Naturally, sir! There could not be the faintest awkwardness between Mrs Gwyn and myself. (In a lower voice) But indeed, it is not very considerate to these poor creatures to bring them into court circles, when they should be scrubbing floors!

CHARLES   (Idly) Would you scrub a floor for me, Nelly?

NELL   (Pointedly) For <u>you</u>, I would, Charles.

LOUISE   (Graciously) Then, madame, if you are in need of money when other employments are no longer open to you, you will not be without the means of an honest livelihood.

NELL   Thanking you for your kind concern, madame, but if I am in need of money, I can go and make it in the theatre. I am not pelted with dirt whenever I appear in public!

CHARLES   (Gravely) It displeases me very much that any of my friends should meet with such discourteous treatment.

NELL   (Shaking her head and mimicking his gravity) It is bad, very bad. (Brightening) But Charles, you don't know yet what I came for!

CHARLES   (Fondly) To make a nuisance of yourself, Nelly?

NELL   Partly; but I wanted to ask you for something.

CHARLES   (A shade of weariness passing over his face) If it's money you want, you must speak to the treasurer.

NELL   It's not money.

CHARLES   Or a place, then, there is really nothing at present I have to give.

NELL   (Stamping) It's not.

CHARLES   (Peevishly) What is it, then? You know I hate to be tormented.

>   (NELL comes up close to him and says in a frank, pleading, affectionate manner)

NELL   I want your company at night, soon! Shall I have it?

CHARLES   (Embracing her tenderly) You shall.

NELL   Then I'll say good-bye to you —

>   (The DUCHESS comes forward and makes a very fine ironical curtsey. NELL steps forward also and when the other has finished, she makes a similar curtsey but in

a much-exaggerated form. The DUCHESS turns her
back.)

(Sings to exit. Humorously, not sentimentally) Remember the
vows that you made to your Nelly. Remember the bower where
you vowed to be true, etc.

> (CHARLES leads NELL to the door and as she is going
> out he pulls her back for a last kiss. When she has gone,
> he turns without much enthusiasm to the DUCHESS.)

LOUISE   (Tearfully) It would be useless for me to ask that I
might be spared such insults for the future. If you loved and
respected me, you would not permit that creature to come into
my presence!

CHARLES   (Bluntly) Is it worse for Nelly to come into your
presence, than for you to come into my wife's?

LOUISE   I have never insulted Her Majesty…

CHARLES   (Startled) I should hope not!

LOUISE   Surely you must see the difference?

CHARLES   All the difference in the world. A lady of your
breeding would be incapable of causing the Queen the slightest
uneasiness. Nelly is a wild thing who doesn't know any better.

LOUISE (Indignantly) That is the excuse you men always
make for your trulls; they understand good behaviour as well as
anyone, but they know their impudence amuses, so they give
free rein to it; and you excuse them and yourselves by saying
they don't know any better. You'd be surprised at the wonderful
improvement a month in Bridewell would make in Mrs Gwyn's
manners!

CHARLES   But I like her best as she is!

LOUISE (Melting) That is what is so hard to bear! I did not regard the sacrifice I made by remaining in your court in this ambiguous position, while I thought I had some power over your heart —

CHARLES My dear, you have the power to make me confoundedly miserable, as well as the happiest of men. If I had the same power over you, I know which I should be the prouder of.

(THEY embrace)

CHARLES (Changing the subject) Has my brother spoken to you about his concert this evening?

LOUISE No, he has not; is he going to invite me to it?

CHARLES Yes, if you would like to go.

LOUISE (Archly) I should like to go – if you don't object?

CHARLES O, James is the last man I could ever be jealous of! He has such a passion for ugly women, I could trust you with him in perfect safety. I sometimes think his mistresses are given to him by his confessor as a penance…

LOUISE (Laughing) His Highness is so severe in his manners and his friends are so – so homely, one would never imagine him to be a man of pleasure!

CHARLES That's very true; and the reason I am put down as a monster of wickedness while he passes for a man of exemplary morals, is that I appear to enjoy myself and he doesn't. The Puritans can forgive anything except light-heartedness.

(Here CHIFFINCH opens the closet door and ushers in the DUKE OF YORK)

There you are, brother. Haven't you some scheme for this evening that you wanted to consult Lady Portsmouth about?

YORK   (Bowing very low) If she will honour me. The idea was to have a small concert in my apartments and supper afterwards; nothing wearisome, you understand, all quite impromptu.

LOUISE   Just what I like!

(YORK bows again)

YORK   (Pathetically) I know you have no opinion of my taste, brother; but as Lady Portsmouth is to be with us may I hope you will join us?

CHARLES   (Kindly) You do me an injustice, James. Your little entertainments are delightful, but I can't avail myself of this one; I'm having supper with the Queen.

YORK   Couldn't you join us after supper?

CHARLES   No, I think not; she particularly wants my company this evening. If Catherine feels inclined, we might visit you in time for one of the songs, but don't expect us.

LOUISE   (Who shows considerable sympathy with YORK, because he is a Roman Catholic, an advocate of ruthless absolutism, and also uniformly stately and polite) Has Your Royal Highness any interesting entries for Newmarket?

YORK   I'm not running a horse this time; I'm leaving the field clear for the King. Are you riding yourself, brother?

CHARLES   Yes. I can't bear to stand by and see somebody else riding Brown Boy; I know he goes more kindly for me than for anybody. To me, the pleasure of racing is riding rather than betting.

LOUISE   Brown Boy! Well, I shall bet on him.

YORK   You shouldn't put your money on a horse, Lady Portsmouth, without asking who the sire was.

LOUISE   (Prettily) Well, Charles, who was your horse's sire?

CHARLES   (Laughing) The sire, madame, had the honour of bestowing his nickname on your humble servant. He was a very fine black stallion called Old Rowley!

> (CHARLES roars with laughter; YORK looks down his nose, and LOUISE looks angry)

LOUISE   In France, a person would lose his ears for such a joke. I wonder you can make anyone respect you when you have no idea what is due to yourself.

YORK   I think, madame, my brother is not deficient in majesty.

CHARLES   Thank you, James. I don't consider my natural children a reproach to me; if only I could have had a boy in wedlock! (Kindly, to YORK) Still, James, I am not without an heir; and since the loss must be mine, I am glad the gain should be yours.

YORK   (Miserably) I know how often you must wish that the Duke of Monmouth could be in my shoes.

CHARLES   (Firmly) No, James. To wish I had a lawful son is one thing; to want a bastard to come after me and dispossess the heir to the English crown, is quite another. You've always been loyal and kind to me, and since I've no heir of my body, I won't repine that I'm to be succeeded by my father's son.

> (YORK kisses his hand)

LOUISE   When does the Duke of Monmouth return?

CHARLES   (Joyously) He should be here early next week.
You've heard of course that the engagement of Bothwell Brig was
a complete routing of the Covenanters' army…

LOUISE   (Smiling delightfully) Of course I have heard it!
What delight you take in speaking of your son's achievement!

CHARLES   Well, well, I mustn't become tedious over it; but
the Londoners certainly expect him next Tuesday or Wednesday;
the bonfires are preparing already and a deputation has waited
on the Lord Mayor to ask for special arrangements to welcome
him.

YORK   (Enviously) He certainly knows his way into the
people's hearts.

CHARLES   (Involuntarily) God bless him! But he mustn't
be allowed to cut too big a figure under the nose of the heir
apparent, brother. Just let the first tide of rejoicings subside, and
we'll send Master Jamie back into private life for a while.

LOUISE   Lord Shaftesbury is saying very kind things about the
Duke of Monmouth.

CHARLES   Is he? That's very distressing!

YORK   Perhaps his lordship means to trim his sails a little – he
is always notoriously disloyal to the King and me.

LOUISE   The Duke of Monmouth is so charming, I am not
surprised that even Lord Shaftesbury should fall under his spell.

CHARLES   (Who has been listening intently) You think Lord
Shaftesbury <u>has</u> fallen under it?

LOUISE   After all, it is not impossible, is it? Lord Shaftesbury is only human.

YORK   (Bitterly) James Fitzroy is a Protestant, and the King's son. It would suit Lord Shaftesbury very well to see him replace me in the succession. Indeed, brother, there is a great deal to be said for making him your heir.

CHARLES   O, everything in the world, except that he's <u>not</u> my heir. But you're mistaken, James. Shaftesbury doesn't want a Protestant successor; he wants a republic.

LOUISE   (Astounded) A republic!! Dear Charles! What are you saying! Are you sure of this?

CHARLES   (Calmly) Perfectly.

LOUISE   But he can never have said so!

CHARLES   Not yet.

YORK   (Groaning) How have we offended God that our race should be so accursed! Our great-grandmother, the Queen of Scots, our noble father…

CHARLES   (Gaily) You are not going to add your noble brother, I hope! Come, James, don't be low-spirited.

YORK   It is difficult to preserve one's cheerfulness, sir, when we have to contend with —

(BRUCE opens the gallery door, tentatively)

BRUCE   Sir, I beg Your Majesty's pardon for this intrusion; but Lord Shaftesbury says he must see Your Majesty for a moment if possible.

CHARLES   (Annoyed) I thought he was to come this evening?

BRUCE   (Distressed) Yes, sire: I told his lordship Your Majesty did not expect him till then: but he says —

CHARLES   O very well; show him in!

> (SHAFTESBURY enters; deferential, smiling, and rubbing his hands at the prospect of making at least three people very uncomfortable)

Do you wish to see me privately, my lord?

SHAFTESBURY   O dear no, sire: I would not ask such trusted confidants of Your Majesty to withdraw, by any means.

CHARLES   (Who has thrown himself into one of the chairs in the middle of the room) What is the matter now, my lord? '

SHAFTESBURY   It is merely, sire, that I thought Your Majesty should have, at the earliest possible moment, the news which has been brought to me.

CHARLES   (Carelessly) Yes?

SHAFTESBURY   The House of Commons has refused the grant for the new ships, Your Majesty.

CHARLES   (After a slight pause: negligently) Oh. Why?

SHAFTESBURY   (With great delicacy but obvious relish) They say, sire, that so much money is being spent (with a sideways glance at LOUISE) on various chargeable ladies about the court – and for another thing; they are afraid that if they did vote the new ships, those ships might be used against the Dutch, and in the French interest: instead of, as devout Protestants would wish, for the Dutch and against the French.

CHARLES   (Idly) That's all one to me, my lord. I don't want the ships. How they can get on without ships, they'd better try and find out.

SHAFTESBURY   (Disappointed) I am very glad the matter

doesn't distress Your Majesty. I was afraid so material a point might have caused Your Majesty some concern.

CHARLES   Not in the least.

SHAFTESBURY   (Becoming more plainly spiteful) Then, sire, they have, I am sorry to say, been very ungracious about His Highness the Duke of York.

(YORK stiffens)

CHARLES   What have they said about poor James?

SHAFTESBURY   (Gleefully) Of course, sire, it's most distressing to a man of my loyalty and feeling: but the fact is: as His Highness is so devout a Catholic, and the anti-Catholic sentiment of the nation is so strong – they don't want him to succeed Your Majesty, when the unhappy moment shall arrive.

CHARLES   (Reasonably) Whom would they like to succeed me? If they can persuade the Lord to work a miracle for me as he did for Abraham, and raise me up a son out of due time, I shall be heartily obliged to them.

SHAFTESBURY   Well, sire: there are ways by which the affair might be managed.

CHARLES   Not that I know of.

SHAFTESBURY   (Bluntly) Your Majesty might divorce the Queen – a second marriage would perhaps produce a son. Of course I feel exceedingly awkward in touching on such a subject – in such society. (Bows to YORK)

CHARLES   (Quietly) Perhaps that was why you asked His Highness to remain?

SHAFTESBURY   (Laughing in a deprecating manner) I know

Your Majesty is not serious there.

CHARLES   (Brusquely) I can't divorce the Queen. I've treated her too badly as it is.

SHAFTESBURY   There is another way – but perhaps the time 'tis scarcely ripe to speak of it.

CHARLES   Then let us spare ourselves the trouble of mentioning it, whatever it may be.

SHAFTESBURY   Certainly, sire. I will take my leave; with renewed apologies for having encroached upon Your Majesty's valuable time.

> (He bows himself out)

> (CHARLES has sunk so low into his chair that he appears to be half-asleep. LOUISE is on his right, YORK on his left.)

LOUISE   (Passionately) That monster!

CHARLES   (Tolerantly) Come, come, my dear. You aren't speaking of the Lord Chancellor, surely?

YORK   Sir, I am distressed to see you so harassed.

> (CHARLES looks at him out of one eye) Can we do anything to amuse you?

LOUISE   (Prettily) Would you like to dance in the gallery?

YORK   A brisk canter before dinner.

LOUISE   Or a game of cards?

CHARLES   I am much obliged to you both. But as a matter of fact, I am playing a game of chess.

LOUISE   (Surprised) Indeed, sir? (She looks round for the pieces)

YORK   With whom, brother?

CHARLES   With Lord Shaftesbury. Oh yes. It has been going on for some time now. Very interesting. Very, very interesting.

(His head falls forward on his chest and he just murmurs)

Very interesting.

CURTAIN

ACT II

SCENE I

The same scene, two days later.

> (CHARLES is examining a spaniel's foot.
> CHIFFINCH stands behind him holding a tray with a
> basin and bandages. BRUCE enters.)

BRUCE   Why, Your Majesty! Is the dog hurt? What has happened?

CHARLES   He trod on a cinder out of one of the Duke of Monmouth's confounded bonfires!

CHIFFINCH   Some ladies have had their shoes burned in the same way.

CHARLES   Well, the Duke must make them amends, but poor Pompey won't be consoled so easily.

BRUCE   (Eagerly) Shall I put the bandage on, sire?

CHARLES   I don't think he'll let anyone but me touch it. Poor dog! What a devil of a thing to happen.

CHIFFINCH   They say the wind blew the embers all over the streets.

CHARLES   They'll start another great fire if they aren't careful. There! How's that, Pompey?

BRUCE   I think he's imposing on you, sir.

> (CHIFFINCH carries the tray into the closet and
> returns)

CHARLES (Holding the dog in his arms) Don't be hard-hearted, Bruce; wait till you've got burned yourself. (To CHIFFINCH) Take him to his basket in my bedroom.

[45]

(Exit CHIFFINCH, with dog)

By the way, Bruce, you were very indiscreet with Lord Shaftesbury t'other morning.

BRUCE   (Distressed) I beg pardon, sire. Did – did his lordship complain of my impertinence?

CHARLES   His lordship congratulated me on having a gentleman who was so zealous in his duties, and so ardent in his devotion to my person. You'll find yourself in the Tower, if you don't take care, Bruce. I don't say I couldn't get you out, but it would be cursedly tiresome to me to have to do it. You might think of that, next time you're inclined to be severe on the Lord Chancellor.

(A faint knock is heard at the door)

BRUCE   (Overcome) I am so very sorry, sire. I —

CHARLES   (Laughing kindly) Never mind, Bruce. See who that is.

(BRUCE opens the gallery door, and discloses the QUEEN, a small, pleasant-looking creature, now standing timidly on the threshold)

BRUCE   (Starting back and bowing very low) Sire, Her Majesty the Queen.

CHARLES   (Surprised and welcoming) Catherine! You wanted me?

(The QUEEN looks uncertainly at BRUCE)

You may go, Bruce.

(Exit BRUCE)

(CHARLES comes forward and takes her by the

hand. His manner shows that he is kind, courteous, affectionate, everything but in love)

QUEEN   (Half panting) I was at cards, Charles – I ran away to you as soon as I heard what they were saying —

CHARLES   What was that, my dear? Come, sit down.

(He tries to lead her to a seat, but she falls down on her knees)

QUEEN   Charles! What can I do?

(She begins to sob; he raises her and makes her sit down in the chair by the hearth, standing over her)

(At last) I know, I have always known, that I am a disappointment to you; but I love you, nobody among them all loves you more than I do.

CHARLES   My dear, I know that you love me, far better than I deserve.

QUEEN   (Desperately) You believe in my devotion?

CHARLES   I should be an ungrateful brute if I did not. How can you ask it?

QUEEN   And that I would die, rather than hurt you...

CHARLES   Don't talk of dying! It would be the only thing you'd ever done that disobliged me...

(She smiles through her tears and lays her cheek against his hand)

QUEEN   I know that I'm not beautiful nor interesting: I'm a poor creature and my children die before they are born. I would have died gladly to give you a son. I've sometimes wanted to die because I couldn't give you one.

CHARLES   (In dismay) My dear —

QUEEN   But at least you do believe that I love you with all my heart and soul and that you have no more loyal and devoted subject than your wife.

CHARLES   Catherine, I am a bad husband...

QUEEN   No, no...

CHARLES   But at least I can value a good wife, the best and kindest a man ever had. What is it that is troubling you? (She bursts into tears)

QUEEN   It is the cruelty of what they say, I don't care about the danger to myself. You may take my life with pleasure, but don't believe me guilty!

CHARLES   My dear, if you go on at this rate, I shall believe you to be very silly. Take your life! (He shakes her gently) Kate! Kate! Have you taken leave of your senses? This is Charles, your husband, your ugly black boy. Who do you think I am? Look at me. (He wipes her eyes) Now come on, out with it.

QUEEN   I won't cry. I know how tiresome women are who make scenes. But ... they are saying in the city, some of them, Lady Denham heard of it, and so did my secretary and he says Mr Chiffinch has heard it too, perhaps he's told you already – if he hasn't, he will, and of course it's quite right he should – you ought to know, that they say I'm trying to poison you.

CHARLES   That you're trying to poison me! Upon my word, Kate, I don't know who is the more absurd – they, or you!

QUEEN   They mean to ruin me, Charles.

CHARLES   But where's their evidence?

QUEEN   They will – find it. I am in danger because I am innocent. If I were guilty, I might escape, as any criminal might, but when they mean to pull an innocent person down, the charges are made conclusive.

CHARLES   You speak, Kate, as if there were no such thing as law and justice.

QUEEN   They are not always the same thing, are they, dear Charles.

CHARLES   That's better! That's a sign your spirits are returning. But indeed I admit that the laws I have been obliged to pass against Catholics and Nonconformists would stick in the gullet of any just and honest man. (Fiercely) But they shan't touch my wife!

QUEEN   Now I know that you know I'm innocent, I don't care what they do to me.

CHARLES   (Angrily) Nobody shall do anything to you. Put your foolish little mind at rest on that, now and for ever.

QUEEN   But Charles, I am afraid – no! I am not afraid now, but I believe that there is such a determination to part me from you, that nothing can prevent it.

CHARLES   Why?

QUEEN   Lord Shaftesbury and his friends are determined that your brother shan't come after you but he must, if you have a barren wife. If I were out of the way, they could give you a new wife, who would bear you children.

CHARLES   No.

QUEEN   O yes, and I assure you I have sometimes wished it might be so; but I cannot put an end to myself, without sin; and

I would not sin, so that you could put an end to me. I think I might almost welcome some violent course of my enemies, so long as you realised I was innocent.

CHARLES   (Desperately) Catherine, have done with this nonsensical talk! It is not your fault that providence has not seen fit to give us any children.

QUEEN   (Half sadly, half smiling) O, but it is I. Other women can bear you children. Aren't there fourteen beautiful proofs that it is my barrenness, not yours?

CHARLES   Fifteen, Kate, I think fifteen.

QUEEN   I have sinned so often in envying their mothers. I think the happiest time of my life was the one I scarcely remember, when I was ill and wandering, and thought I was in childbed.

CHARLES   (Groans) Catherine!

QUEEN   You cried, Charles, didn't you? I do remember that.

CHARLES   I did.

QUEEN   And you begged me not to die; it was that that made me get well, I think. (Sighs) It would have been better in the end if you'd left me alone.

CHARLES   (In agony) You are making me hate myself —

QUEEN   (Contritely) O! I never meant it…

CHARLES   (Taking her hand) I know, it is your not meaning to hurt me that does hurt me.

QUEEN   I mustn't be melancholy. Besides, I am so proud of your protection.

(CHARLES kisses her forehead)

CHARLES   It is your right, but you shall have it enforced with every show of my love and gratitude.

QUEEN   I must take my leave, if you will excuse me, dear Charles.

CHARLES   Who is waiting on you?

QUEEN   Lady Denham, poor thing, she will have been very uncomfortable in the ante-room; that chimney smokes so!

(CHARLES pulls the bell)

CHARLES   Well, I may have a smoking chimney, but I haven't got the other half of the curse – a railing wife!

QUEEN   (Laughing) Aren't you absurd!

(CHIFFINCH enters from the closet door)

CHARLES   Chiffinch, tell Lady Denham Her Majesty is coming out.

(CHIFFINCH goes out of the other door, and is heard calling: 'Lady Denham to Her Majesty!')

(Quietly) No more fears, Kate, of me or anyone.

QUEEN   (Standing on tiptoe and whispering) None of you, and therefore none of anyone!

(CHIFFINCH re-enters, holds the door open and bows)

(Walking very erect and proudly, and speaking gaily and graciously:) Mr Chiffinch! You have heard these rumours of my trying to poison His Majesty? His Majesty has expressed confidence in my innocence, and absolutely forbidden me to pay any further attention to them.

CHIFFINCH (Bowing) So I should suppose, Your Majesty.

(Exit QUEEN)

CHARLES Chiffinch. Do you know anything about these stories?

CHIFFINCH Well, sir, I heard something of them yesterday for the first time. Of course, nobody inside the palace could be expected to give them any credit, but...

CHARLES But outside! Any stick will do to beat the Catholics. Chiffinch, it must be known at once that the Queen is under my special protection, not only as my wife but as my friend. We must arrange a series of public appearances immediately.

CHIFFINCH Yes, sir, but I should not imagine that the opposition would have even hoped that anything would have come of this. It's just one of their little tricks.

CHARLES I'm not so sure, and in the present state of things even a merry little joke like this may become serious. What troubles me, though, is they think I hold the Queen so slightly that I shan't protect her, they think I'll snatch at the opportunity of getting another wife. That's my fault.

CHIFFINCH Surely not, sir. I should say it was theirs.

CHARLES It's their mistake, certainly. It's the Puritan legacy, they think that a man who is a little free with women is capable of any villainy.

CHIFFINCH If they judge by their own leader, they're quite right. Lord Shaftesbury was the biggest whoremaster in England till he got this ulcer in his side, and he's capable of anything under heaven.

CHARLES   I think so. Not that I blame him for his amorous adventures. I don't think God will be hard on a man for taking a little pleasure out of the way! To my mind malice and cruelty are the sins against the Holy Ghost.

CHIFFINCH   Undoubtedly, sire.

CHARLES   To accuse the Queen!

CHIFFINCH   When Your Majesty makes it plain that you see through that, they'll be held up; their impeachment of the Queen is the only way to debar the Duke of York.

CHARLES   I hope to God you're right!

(A noise of talking and laughing, off)

CHIFFINCH   I imagine the Duke of Monmouth is approaching. sire.

(He sets the gallery door open and retires through the closet)

(CHARLES takes a turn about the room and stands with his back to the fire. At that moment there appears at the gallery door the DUKE OF MONMOUTH; he is a weak-looking but exceedingly beautiful young man, who wears a periwig of brown hair lighter than his father's. He is dressed with the utmost richness in a suit of cloth of gold and he enters on the scene as if he were the god of day. CHARLES no sooner catches sight of him than he comes.)

CHARLES   Jamie, my boy! I'm glad to see you.

MONMOUTH   Dad!

(He kisses CHARLES's hand, and CHARLES throws

his other arm around him)

CHARLES   I've not had a word with you since you arrived. I was pleased, Jamie, so pleased and proud.

MONMOUTH   (Importantly) You had all the despatches, of course?

CHARLES   Yes, I read them all. You didn't write any of them yourself, I notice?

(CHARLES sits down in the chair nearest the hearth; MONMOUTH half kneels on the other, resting his arms on its back)

MONMOUTH   (Ingenuously) Why, Dad, I can't write very well. I'm not like you, you know! I've never properly got the hang of it. And there are always secretaries.

CHARLES   But what do you do when you are writing to a lady? Use a secretary?

MONMOUTH   O, I can manage a line or two.

CHARLES   You didn't manage half a line to me! Not even your duty to your old Dad at the bottom of one of Sir Stephen Walmsley's despatches!

MONMOUTH   (Laughing) Zounds, Dad! Can you see old Wormy's face if I'd said, 'Put my duty to my Dad in your next letter, Sir Stephen.' He looks as if he had the belly-ache if anyone reminds him by a word or a look that I'm your boy.

CHARLES   God rot him!

MONMOUTH   (Generously) Still, he's a useful man. He did his duty at Bothwell Brig.

CHARLES   And you did yours, Jamie. I'll wager it put life into them all to see your handsome face at the head of the line, my darling.

MONMOUTH   (Vaingloriously) O, they like me. I get that from you, Dad. I couldn't resist giving Wormy a dig or two. He praised the way I helped one of the troopers to doctor his horse. 'I am glad,' says Wormy in his sour way, 'that Your Grace has the art of making friends with those you lead.' And I said, as grave as a judge: 'His Majesty has taught me that, from my cradle.'

(He laughs, and CHARLES also)

CHARLES   And you were not hurt at all?

MONMOUTH   Not a scratch. The whole expedition went without a hitch. Luck was with us from the very start.

CHARLES   (Shrewdly) What would you have done if it had been against you? (He brings out his pocket-book and pencil and goes with his usual swift movement to the table) Look! Show me what your tactics would have been if the Covenanters' line hadn't given way at that scaur above the bridge?

MONMOUTH   (Laughing uneasily) You've got it all in your head, haven't you, sir?

CHARLES   I read the despatches, you see. (He is obviously waiting for MONMOUTH to draw a diagram)

MONMOUTH   (Taking up pencil) Well, here's the enemy...

CHARLES   (Encouragingly) Yes.

MONMOUTH   And here's the bridge.

CHARLES   Good.

MONMOUTH   And here... (making marks)

CHARLES   What are those? Cows?

MONMOUTH   The Covenanters' ranks; you see (pause)
to tell the truth, the more successful type of commander never
does know what he's going to do till he comes to do it. So many
considerations guide his course, which can only be understood
at the actual moment; the element of uncertainty…

CHARLES   Of course there is an element of uncertainty; but I
take it that you had your alternative plan of action somewhere in
your head, in case you'd lost the first engagement?

MONMOUTH   (Haughtily) I regret that Your Majesty is
not satisfied with my services. I understood that it was enough
to win the battle and, incidentally, the campaign; not that I
should be expected to fight the engagement over again with Your
Majesty on a purely hypothetical basis.

CHARLES   (Gets up and slaps him on the back, to the great
damage of MONMOUTH's dignified position) Hypothetical
fiddlesticks! Jamie! Why don't you say straight out 'I'd no plan
in this chuckle-head of mine, and I relied on old Wormsmeat
to tell me what to do if I gave out?' Bless you, my boy. You've
come home with victory, for which I thank God; and unhurt,
for which I'm even more thankful. Look cheerful, my son. I've a
little present for you. (He goes to the hearth and rings the bell)

MONMOUTH   (Brightening) A present?

(Enter CHIFFINCH)

CHARLES   Is Pumphrey there?

CHIFFINCH   Waiting, Your Majesty.

CHARLES   Bring him in.

(Exit CHIFFINCH)

MONMOUTH   (His gaiety restored) Do you know, Dad, ever

since those old days in the Hague, when you were always buying me whips and trumpets and gingerbread, I never see you after an absence without wondering what you've got for me in your pocket!

CHARLES   You shall see.

(CHIFFINCH brings in MR PUMPHREY, the KING's clockmaker, who is staggering under the weight of a very ornate and beautiful clock, which he is obliged to put down on the table before he can make his bow)

CHARLES   Well, Pumphrey, here's the Duke back again.

PUMPHREY   Yes, indeed Your Majesty, so I have the happiness to see. I praise God for His Grace's safe return. The whole of London is talking of His Grace's remarkable feats of arms!

> (The KING looks pleased; then he comes forward to the table. MONMOUTH approaches it from the other side. PUMPHREY stands to the left)

CHARLES   So, there it is.

PUMPHREY   A wonderful example, Your Majesty! Swiss works and the case from Paris.

MONMOUTH   (Delighted) Is this for me?

CHARLES   It is if you like it.

MONMOUTH   It's exactly what I want most! You can't get them made in England like this. (To PUMPHREY) I've always coveted the one like it the King has in his dressing-room.

CHARLES   (Drily) It's a wonder it's still there then! Have you a glass, Pumphrey?

(PUMPHREY produces a magnifying glass and gives it to the KING with a bow)

Let me see what he's done here…

MONMOUTH   (Urgently) Don't take it to pieces, Dad! (To PUMPHREY) The King takes every clock in the palace to bits.

PUMPHREY   (Blandly) O, but His Majesty can put them together again as well as any clockmaker.

CHARLES   (Absorbed) Very, very pretty. Let's hear the chime.

(He stirs the clock up; MONMOUTH makes a movement as if to prevent him)

PUMPHREY   (Blandly) Your Grace need have no fear. Your Grace may repose every confidence in His Majesty.

(The clock strikes with a sweet, icy chime)

MONMOUTH   What a strange chime! Like the stroke of fate.

CHARLES   The stroke of fate?

MONMOUTH   So sharp and clear. But it's charming.

PUMPHREY   The Swiss chimes are harsher than the French, Your Grace, but if these are not mellow enough, they can be softened down.

MONMOUTH   No, leave them as they are. What a lovely piece of work! Perfect…

CHARLES   Just one thing needed: your cypher on the centre panel; in pearls, eh?

MONMOUTH   (Eagerly) Or diamonds!

CHARLES   Pearls would be more in keeping with the design; how about pearls with turquoises?

PUMPHREY   I was about to observe, when His Majesty took the words out of my mouth, that turquoises would take up the colour of the enamel to admiration.

(CHARLES sees that MONMOUTH looks disappointed)

CHARLES   Well, my boy, it's your clock, let it be diamonds then. (To PUMPHREY) But don't make it more costly than you can help. It's not that I grudge the money, but it's only that I haven't got it.

PUMPHREY   Perfectly, Your Majesty. I understand exactly what is required. It shall be put in hand immediately.

MONMOUTH   Bring it home the instant it's ready…

CHARLES   Yes, Pumphrey, see it's brought straight to me as soon as it arrives.

PUMPHREY   Certainly, Your Majesty.

(Exit with the clock)

MONMOUTH   (Kindly) Are you short of money, Dad?

CHARLES   A difficult time is coming, and I'm laying by what I can. (Cheerfully) However, I can pay for your new clock, whatever happens.

MONMOUTH   My clock! I wish he hadn't got to take it away the first moment I have it!

(CHARLES has walked to the hearth and is kicking the fire with his heel)

CHARLES   (Reminiscently) That's your mother's impatience coming out in you.

MONMOUTH   (Looking up sharply – glad of this lead) Yes – I daresay.

(There is a pause)

(Dramatically) Father!

CHARLES   (At the unusual form of address, the KING turns round sharply) What's the matter?

MONMOUTH (Leaning over the table and speaking with a mixture of hesitation and audacity) I suppose – you never married my mother?

CHARLES   (Astounded) Married your mother?

MONMOUTH   But you were very fond of her?

CHARLES   Very fond, and very grateful to her. She made me very happy; and when she found other protectors whose pockets were better lined than mine, why, poor girl, she was welcome to her luck.

MONMOUTH   (Ignoring the last sentence) But when you did love her – wouldn't it have been a natural thing to marry her?

CHARLES   When I met your mother, I was in exile, but I was already the King of England. She was a play actress touring the Low Countries.

MONMOUTH   And you thought the alliance was impossible!

CHARLES   I never thought about it at all, and neither did she. Jamie, what are you driving at?

MONMOUTH   Didn't King Edward IV marry the widow of a shopkeeper?

CHARLES   How did you know that?

MONMOUTH   (Airily) Really, sir, isn't it one of the commonplaces of English history?

CHARLES   And since when have <u>you</u> known the commonplaces of English history? Come! When did Edward IV ascend the throne? Perhaps you can tell me that?

MONMOUTH   (Taken aback, weakly) Well, I suppose it was some time before your father…

CHARLES   (Drily) It hasn't been after, to my knowledge. (Sharply) Once more, what are you driving at?

MONMOUTH   (Boldly) There is a certain feeling about, that if enquiries were made, it might come to light that you had married my mother.

CHARLES   (Coming towards him, and speaking half-humorously, half-grimly) Shall I tell you what might also come to light? It might come to light that you're the son of Lord Algernon Sidney.

MONMOUTH   What?

CHARLES   O yes, your dear mother hated to be cruel to anybody; he admired her quite as much as I did. There are plenty of people to say you're not my son at all.

MONMOUTH   (Winningly) Do <u>you</u> believe that, Dad?

CHARLES   (Abruptly) No.

     (BOTH laugh)

MONMOUTH   Nobody would make <u>me</u> believe it, when I remember how you used to play with me. You were a wonderful father.

CHARLES   (Melting, and glad to change the subject) Do you remember how I nearly cracked your skull by tossing you up to the ceiling? You just looked at me in a woebegone manner, but you never made a sound.

MONMOUTH   It didn't hurt very much!

CHARLES   It did, my boy. Your poor little face was as white as a sheet; I thought I'd killed you when I heard the crack; but you were always as brave as a young lion.

MONMOUTH   You love me, don't you? (Matter-of-factedly, not sentimentally)

CHARLES   Haven't I shown it?

MONMOUTH   (Uneasily) Yes, yes, of course. But shouldn't you like to see me in the position of your son?

CHARLES   You mean of my heir? What's the use of wishing the impossible?

MONMOUTH   Why is it impossible?

CHARLES   Since you know so many of the commonplaces of history I'm surprised you need to be told that the English crown goes by legitimate descent; it isn't bequeathed at the pleasure of the reigning sovereign, like a pair of candlesticks or a salt cellar.

MONMOUTH   But...

CHARLES   (Pettishly) But <u>what</u>?

MONMOUTH   You could <u>tell</u> the people I am legitimate —

CHARLES   (With growing impatience) How can I tell them you're legitimate when you're not?

MONMOUTH   If you said so, they'd believe it...

CHARLES   O no, they wouldn't. The English people aren't damned fools, whatever <u>you</u> may be —

MONMOUTH   (Heatedly) Lord Shaftesbury isn't a fool...
(He stops, realising what he has said)

(There is a long pause)

CHARLES   At last! I've been waiting for that. So it's Lord Shaftesbury who's been giving you your history lessons!

MONMOUTH   (Earnestly) sir, I swear I...

CHARLES   Jamie, I warn you; you'd better leave all this alone.

MONMOUTH   (Eagerly) Forgive me. I never meant any harm, nothing was farther from my thoughts. You must know that, sir. It's only that I can't help sometimes remembering my beautiful mother...

CHARLES   (Rudely) Then perhaps you remember your beautiful mother throwing a frying-pan at you?

MONMOUTH   (With dignity) I daresay I was very troublesome to her.

CHARLES   Not half so troublesome as you look like being to me.

MONMOUTH   I would never do anything to hurt you, Dad!

CHARLES   That's not what I'm afraid of. You'll run your neck into a noose and I shan't be able to save you.

MONMOUTH   I swear I won't, Dad.

(CHARLES looks at him without speaking)

I swear I'm absolutely innocent of anything. I swear that nothing could make up to me for losing your favour, I promise solemnly.

CHARLES   Jamie! You're not a clever man. So don't make friends with clever men; they'd have you at a disadvantage.

MONMOUTH   (Offended) Thank you for the advice.

CHARLES   My poor boy, I wish you had the sense to profit

by it; but do at least listen to this; Lord Shaftesbury probably omitted to tell you in his history lessons that he was one of the most ardent supporters of Oliver Cromwell.

MONMOUTH   Shaftesbury? A supporter of Cromwell! Surely, sir…

CHARLES   Listen. He's notoriously disloyal to me; and he's about the cleverest man in the kingdom with the possible exception of myself. It's not for my sake, it's for yours that I say – don't have anything to do with him.

(Pause)

MONMOUTH   (Impulsively) I won't, Dad! (He comes and leans against the KING's shoulder) I'd rather be your bastard, whom you love, than a Prince of Wales you didn't love.

CHARLES   (Fondly) Would you? Jamie? (Pause) You'd better be off now; I know you're expected at half-a-dozen places. You've had a royal welcome, haven't you?

MONMOUTH   (Hesitating as the irresistible association of ideas comes across him) Yes…

CHARLES   Get along with you. (He kisses MONMOUTH and pushes him towards the gallery door)

(MONMOUTH, at the door, bows and is about to go out)

Remember what I've said to you.

MONMOUTH   (Gaily) I will, Dad.

(He stands for a second, a radiant figure poised in the doorway; then goes out)

(As the door shuts him off, the KING starts forward

and cries out as if he'd seen him fall over a precipice)

CHARLES Jamie!

(There is a moment's pause; then the closet door opens and BRUCE looks in)

BRUCE Did Your Majesty call?

CHARLES (Recollecting himself) No, no.

(BRUCE is about to depart)

CHARLES Wait, Bruce. I want you to write for me.

(BRUCE opens a drawer from which he takes writing materials, and sits down. CHARLES remains at the hearth and dictates, sufficiently slowly, as he is composing, for BRUCE to take down)

'There being a false and malicious report spread abroad by some, who are neither friends to me nor the Duke of Monmouth, that I was contracted or married to his mother and though I am confident this idle story cannot have any effect in this age, yet I thought it my duty in relation to the true succession of the crown, that no one may have any pretence to make a disturbance on that score, to declare, as I do here declare, in the presence of Almighty God, that I never was contracted to any woman whatsoever but to my wife, Queen Catherine, to whom I am now married. In witness whereof I set my hand...' Thank you. Leave it with me. That's all, Bruce.

(Exit BRUCE)

(CHARLES sits down at the table and draws a large signature on the page; then he throws down the pen with a sigh)

SCENE II

The scene is narrowed down in lighting to a very small space in order to emphasise its intensity; hardly more can be seen than the two figures and the table at which they sit.

> (Facing the audience is LORD SHAFTESBURY on the far side of the table. He leans on it, towards the right, where, on the nearer side, MONMOUTH is sprawling in a chair; the table is covered with bottles, cups and glasses.)

SHAFTESBURY   Let me fill your cup, Your Highness?

MONMOUTH   (Deprecating, but pleased) You mustn't call me that, you know.

SHAFTESBURY   I beg pardon: it slipped out. How natural it sounds! I think you'd find it came very readily to the lips of other people besides myself.

MONMOUTH   (Sighing) I must tell you: the King denies absolutely that he ever married my mother.

SHAFTESBURY   Well, well, that is natural enough, after all.

MONMOUTH   You mean…?

SHAFTESBURY   Consider their relative situations: it would not now be very easy for the King to admit it. Of course, I mean no slight to the excellent lady who had the happiness to be your mother…

MONMOUTH   O don't put yourself out on my account. I know my mother was a whore. Am I to blame her for that? If she hadn't been, I should never have been born at all.

SHAFTESBURY   (Applauding) A very reasonable way of looking at the matter.

[66]

MONMOUTH   And why not? A good many of us might say the same, when all's said and done.

SHAFTESBURY   Undoubtedly. But when Your Highness says that you would never have been born at all, I am not altogether sure that I agree with you.

MONMOUTH   When we spoke of this before, I confess I had hopes that it might turn out to be as you suggest; but His Majesty denies it so positively and frankly, I don't think it a likely thing to have happened in any case —

SHAFTESBURY   (Leaning forward) That is where we join issue. Put the case to yourself. Charles Stuart aged twenty: unbridled passions, no prospects, no hopes. A life of indigence and misery; few friends and no pleasures – save what Love would promise. Your mother, ravishingly lovely and as kind as she was beautiful. May he not very well have thought that the world offered him no happiness but in Lucy Barlow's arms?

MONMOUTH   Yes, but…

SHAFTESBURY   But what! Consider. Your mother's heart he has already made his own, but not her principles! He has conquered her affections but not her chastity; before she consents to make their mutual happiness, she demands…

MONMOUTH   (Shaking his head) That won't do, my lord! I remember my mama quite well; that wasn't her way at all!

SHAFTESBURY   (Not at all nonplussed) Your admirable frankness, sir, emboldens me to give you my real opinion of the subject.

MONMOUTH   (Sitting up) Oh, you've got another theory, then?

SHAFTESBURY   Certainly. Your mother was surrounded by a swarm of place-hunting, time-serving, out-at-elbows fellows, some of whom had gone into exile with the King, but more of whom had been living abroad because they feared the gallows if they came home. Some of these, noting your mother's ascendency over the King, determine to play for a long stake. They represent to her that if she hold off a little farther, she can inflame the King into granting anything, even a legal marriage. That this occurred, I for one am positive.

MONMOUTH   God bless my soul!

SHAFTESBURY   And had the Restoration happened ten years before it did, King Charles II would not have been able to avoid admitting that his young favourite was his lawful heir!

MONMOUTH   (Struck) You put it very convincingly, my lord. (Recollecting himself) But, somehow, it doesn't sound like my father!

SHAFTESBURY   (Ingratiatingly) With your forgiveness, sir, such of us as have observed His Majesty with other eyes than those of a devoted son, may have been able to form – dare I venture to say it? – a wider and juster estimate of His Majesty's character. Your Highness's excellent powers of judgement and penetration are in this case, shall I say wilfully? – blinded – let me fill your glass – blinded by your filial loyalty and affection.

MONMOUTH   The King has always been very kind to me.

SHAFTESBURY   No doubt; the King has many good qualities; that he is a man of great personal charm is proved by the fact that he has kept his throne up till now.

MONMOUTH   (Roused) Really, sir!

SHAFTESBURY   (Plainly) Come, come, Your Grace. When
your father was restored, the people were so mad with delight
they'd have lain down in the street to let his horse walk over
them. The Parliament was so zealous on his behalf that they far
outstripped his desire for revenge, and the punishment of the
regicides was taken out of his hands because they wouldn't bear,
for his own sake, to see him deal leniently with his enemies. In
less than twenty years, what has come about? Today, the temper
of Parliament is so threatening that anybody less incurably
idle and flippant than the King would have taken warning and
pulled himself in. He's on the very brink of a precipice. And
what does he do? He passes his days in a ceaseless round of
extravagant folly and idle merriment; his nights … but I will not
offend the dutifulness of a son by reminding you how his nights
are passed.

MONMOUTH   (Who has been drinking continuously) That's
all very fine, old cock, but how do you pass your own?

SHAFTESBURY   (Laughing) Ha! Ha! Ha! Very good, very
just, I must admit! Your Highness is a man of the world, and my
reputation has not escaped you, I perceive.

MONMOUTH   I shouldn't think it's escaped anybody;
only you're so devilish sly, we never see any of them! I think of
coming down one day to raid your Dorsetshire dovecot, my lord!

SHAFTESBURY   You shall be very welcome, sir, I promise
you. Indeed, one of the things that draws me to Your Highness,
and draws many, disclaim it as modestly as you will, is Your
Highness's blending the qualities of an enlightened patriot
and an upholder of your country's Church, with those of
a brave soldier and a man of fashion and the world. Your
Highness's candour and good breeding have shown me twice

in this interview that I may altogether trust myself to you in open speech; and now I will do so, relying completely on Your Highness's understanding and good sense...

MONMOUTH   (Vaingloriously) You may do that, certainly.

SHAFTESBURY   (Leaning closer) Sir: it is not only I who perceive your unique fitness to ascend the throne; you must have felt, on many occasions, and especially on your return from your splendid victory at Bothwell Brig, that the people put their whole hearts into their welcome of you. The banners, the bonfires, the garlands, the speeches, the bell-ringing, the dancing and rejoicings – it was a civic triumph that recalled the days of Ancient Rome.

MONMOUTH   They made a good show, certainly.

SHAFTESBURY   And have you any doubt, speaking as a man of experience and sense, that those good men who shouted themselves hoarse for you, would shout just as joyfully in your coronation procession (He leans closer to MONMOUTH) whether your mother's marriage certificate had been found or not?

MONMOUTH   (Shrinking back a little) Well, sir; it's a doubtful point, is it not? My mother's marriage certificate wouldn't give me a better pair of arms or legs, or improve my complexion, or sharpen my wits; but it would give me something the people of England seem to set store by; and I'm afraid that if I tried to make myself King without it, I might end up by waiting to take my last little walk on Tower Hill one morning.

SHAFTESBURY   (Shaking his head) You forget, sir, you are the people's darling. Does that give you no power? The mere sight of Your Grace at the head of a troop of household cavalry would draw hundreds to your side.

MONMOUTH   (Nervously) My lord, I hope nobody's likely to overhear you. Walls have ears, and so on, haven't they? Or the people behind them have.

SHAFTESBURY   You need have no fear. You are safe enough. I believe your father devoutly wishes he might say the same.

MONMOUTH   My father's all right, even if they do keep him short of money; after all, he's used to that.

SHAFTESBURY   (Standing up) James Fitzroy, your father is on the verge of destruction. The time is fast approaching when it won't be asked any more whom he married, or whom he begot; he will be swept away into everlasting darkness, as his father was, by a people whose deepest feelings he has outraged and ignored.

MONMOUTH   Good God in heaven, my lord…

SHAFTESBURY   There is one thing, and one only, that fills the popular mind at present, and that is hatred and terror of Catholicism. The common people look back to great national perils which they lay at the door of Rome: the Spanish Armada, the Gunpowder Plot, the Great Fire of London…

MONMOUTH   But it's preposterous! The Great Fire was an accident! A baker's shop…

SHAFTESBURY   Try to explain it as 'an accident' to the London mob, Your Grace. The Church foresees its thousands of clergy dispossessed and driven out to starve, or to perish on the quartering-block; hundreds of the nobility and landed gentry remember only too well that their forefathers received their estates from the spoils of the monasteries at the Reformation and

they know that a re-established Church of Rome will drive them
out of their halls and manors, and hang them up from their own
doorposts if they resist, as King Henry VIII hanged the priors
and abbots. And in spite of all this, the King persists that his heir
is the Catholic Duke of York; he refuses to divorce a Catholic
Queen who can't give him a son; he maintains a French alliance
and is ready to declare himself a Catholic and force Catholicism
on his subjects, if he can thereby get enough money from the
King of France to circumvent his own Parliament; he shows his
enmity to the Dutch republic, that bulwark of Protestantism
in Europe, on every occasion. How long do you suppose this
will be suffered to endure? I tell you, your only chance to save
your father from the fate of Charles I, is to lay hands on him,
shut him safely up, and announce yourself as the Saviour of
Protestantism, and the security of the subject.

MONMOUTH   (Aghast) Lay hands on him – on my father!
But suppose I failed?

SHAFTESBURY   Pshaw. This from the victor of Bothwell
Brig?

MONMOUTH   It's not danger daunts me, it's my conscience.

SHAFTESBURY   Young man, do you value your father's life?
Will you stand by and see him perish, from a mere punctilio?
You are doing this solely in his own interests. And what
objection would a man like your father have to easy retirement?
A pang, no doubt, in greatness going off, but give him a park
to hunt in, a troupe of players to divert him with their bawdry,
cocks to fight, and pretty women to go to bed with, and what
more would Charles Stuart ask of life? He would willingly
relinquish the cares of government, once he was forced, and to a
regent who treated him with the affectionate consideration of a

son! Let him retain the name of King: but let the management of the state rest with him who is fitted to cope with it, with the national hero, young in years but old in judgement: the people's saviour and the people's friend.

(MONMOUTH rises unsteadily to his feet)

MONMOUTH   There's a great deal in what you say – yes – he's been very kind to me. You mustn't do anything to hurt him, you know.

SHAFTESBURY   Your Highness! Can we offer greater security for His Majesty's comfort and safety than by saying that you yourself shall have the ordering of it?

MONMOUTH   (Half drunk) Of course, I shall take every precaution to see to that. That shall be my first thought – I shall take care of that; the people must grant me my father's life…

SHAFTESBURY   When the people know that you have responded to all their wishes, and have stepped forward to save them from the jaws of ruin – what will they refuse you that you like to ask?

MONMOUTH   Yes. I shall take care of that…

(SHAFTESBURY fills his glass and MONMOUTH drinks it off then he falls forward onto the table and slips off it to the floor, where he lies in a drunken stupor. SHAFTESBURY comes round to the front and looks at him, then he laughs soundlessly and turns him over with his foot.)

SCENE III

The Queen's dressing-room, late in the afternoon.

> (The QUEEN, the DUCHESS OF PORTSMOUTH,
> and TWO LADIES (or GENTLEMEN) are playing
> cards; they conclude the game as the scene opens)

LOUISE   Twenty-four guineas. I am really quite distressed,
madame.

QUEEN   It is my own fault. The King has often said how
much he hates gambling, and I am always meaning to stop; but
somehow I – there you are, Duchess.

LOUISE   Thank you, madame.

> (Enter the DUKE OF YORK)

YORK   Good evening, Your Majesty; Duchess, your humble
servant. I hoped I should find the King here.

QUEEN   (Happily) You will. He is coming here as soon as he
gets back from the theatre. You look troubled. is anything the
matter?

> (YORK sits down)

YORK   My secretary has got himself into trouble.

QUEEN   What, poor Mr Coleman?

YORK   Yes. It's this raging insanity for persecuting Catholics.
Some damned spy has been in his lodging and broken open his
desk and discovered some letters!

LOUISE   (Involuntarily) Mon Dieu!

QUEEN   But what letters?

YORK   (Persuasively) My dear sister, you and the Duchess

at least will understand that they were extremely innocent. Coleman is rather foolish, but he's the honestest fellow alive. He has had a correspondent in Rome; as a matter of fact, in the Pope's household.

QUEEN   (Startled) In the Pope's household.

LOUISE   (Defiantly) What is the harm in that, madame?

QUEEN   None, of course, except that the King won't be pleased if anything comes out of the palace just now that is at all awkward. What did the letters say? I hope they were not indiscreet? If they were he was very much to blame, as your secretary.

YORK   How can I blame him for what they said, when they only expressed the dearest wish of my own heart? That this unhappy country could return to the Mother Church.

LOUISE   (Eagerly) They discussed the reconversion of England to Catholicism?

QUEEN   How very unfortunate!

LOUISE   Unfortunate, madame?

QUEEN   That they should have been discovered just now. I am afraid His Majesty will be very angry.

YORK   That is why I wanted to explain to him in your presence, my dear sister; under your protection, as it were, and the Duchess's also, if she will be so good. I know that secretly you have every sympathy with Coleman.

QUEEN   I have great sympathy with him, poor man, but his duty, and ours for that matter, is to the King. Still, if you feel, brother, that our presence is any protection to you, we shall be very glad to lend it to you.

LOUISE   Indeed, yes.

YORK   I am deeply grateful… I don't look forward to making this known to the King, but I'd rather he heard of it from me than from anyone else. O dear! (He groans and buries his head in his hands)

LOUISE   (With great sympathy) Your Highness is worn out!

YORK   (Raising a haggard face) What my brother said of Lord Shaftesbury's wanting a republic is very true. He is determined to get me out of the way.

LOUISE   I know he is an enemy of Your Highness, because you are a Catholic and he is afraid of the country's reverting to the true faith under your rule – but are you sure he wants the King to have no heir?

YORK   (In a low, confidential tone) You think he was concerned in this talk about the possibility of Monmouth's succeeding?

QUEEN   The King thought he was. His Majesty warned the Duke of Monmouth to have nothing to do with him.

LOUISE   So I heard; and a design to put the Duke on the throne doesn't look like republican fervour, does it?

YORK   (With a bitter laugh) My dear Duchess! You haven't got to the bottom of Lord Shaftesbury! The Duke might be King in name, but have you any doubt as to who would be King in fact?

LOUISE   But the very idea is absurd! How could he even set about such a thing?

YORK   (Wretchedly) I don't know: he's a snake in the grass. (He rises and paces about) All I do know is this – his unseen workings are all directed to the ruin of our family. I believe that every public calamity – even every significant event – has Lord Shaftesbury at the bottom of it.

LOUISE   (Sweetly) Indeed, I believe Your Highness exaggerates; as a matter of fact, I dined with Lord Shaftesbury today.

QUEEN & YORK   You did, Duchess? Did you, indeed?

LOUISE   O, I know he's not altogether a pleasant man —

YORK   As full of treachery as an egg is full of meat!

LOUISE   But he was so pressing: and I thought perhaps, if poor I could make a friend of him, what an advantage it might be to the King?

QUEEN   (Blandly) Always thoughtful for others, Duchess.

LOUISE   (Serenely) I try to be, madame.

YORK   (Bitterly) I have no doubt that his lordship was at his most amiable in entertaining so fair a lady; but I doubt if even your charms, Duchess, will succeed in inducing him to leave off persecuting the Catholics. Why, have you heard the newest thing? There's a man called Titus Oates who says he's discovered a Catholic Plot against the King's life —

QUEEN   O, Charles would laugh at that —

YORK   He may laugh, but any slander of the Catholics is seized upon by this sinful and degenerate people.

LOUISE   O but surely nobody would take Titus Oates seriously! I've seen him.

BOTH   Have you? When? Where?

LOUISE   Why, at Lord Shaftesbury's, some of the aldermen

had brought him; I arrived just as he was being shown out of the door.

YORK   What sort of a man is he?

LOUISE   O, perfectly ridiculous; he has no neck, and his chin is half as long as his face, and I believe he squints.

YORK   And what had Lord Shaftesbury to say to him?

LOUISE   O, nothing at all; he had been brought to Lord Shaftesbury because he had been making these wild assertions; but I fancy we shan't hear any more of him. How could anyone take such a creature as that seriously, you know?

> (Enter CHARLES. The KING wears his hat and looks very merry. He kisses first the QUEEN's hand, then the DUCHESS's, and throws himself down on a seat)

QUEEN   Was the play amusing, Charles?

CHARLES   Exceedingly; I've seen it before, but it makes me laugh more every time I see it.

LOUISE   What was it, sir?

CHARLES   The Country Wife. What a dog that Wycherley is!

> (He laughs and the QUEEN laughs also)

LOUISE   (Primly) I believe, sir, that if the ladies laugh at it, they forfeit their reputations as modest women.

QUEEN   O dear. Have I done wrong then?

CHARLES   My wife is too innocent to understand why she shouldn't laugh.

YORK   Alas, Duchess! Hadn't you better laugh now?

LOUISE   And so I do, over such a to-do about nothing. Isn't that one of Shakespeare's plays?

CHARLES   I don't know, Duchess. I have never read any of Shakespeare's plays. My father was very fond of reading them; but somehow they have never come my way.

YORK   But brother, you have surely read one or two? Hamlet, now, I am sure you have read Hamlet.

CHARLES   No, I have not, brother; but as you know, my education was very much neglected. The years that my father had me with him in camp I never opened a book if I could help it; and afterwards (he sighs) ah, afterwards I was learning from other masters. On the whole, I don't regret it. Greek and Latin are very gentlemanly accomplishments, but I think that in the modern world one wants something else.

LOUISE   Your Majesty is one of the most accomplished sovereigns in Europe.

(CHARLES kisses her hand)

YORK   (Nervously) Brother, I fear I must trouble you with something.

CHARLES   (Peevishly) Indeed! Then don't let us bore the ladies with it. Come into my dressing-room.

YORK   The truth is I should like them to be present. I know they sympathise with my distress.

CHARLES   What the devil is it?

YORK   My secretary, Coleman, has, I am afraid, got himself into serious trouble.

CHARLES   (Sitting up) Your secretary Coleman! You don't say you've still got that man with you? I told you to dismiss him months ago.

YORK   I know, brother. I should have done so immediately. I told him, in fact, that he was to go, that it was your wish. But, poor honest man! He was so grieved at leaving my service, I allowed him a little while to find a new employment, and now...

CHARLES   (Impatiently) And now what? I needn't ask – he's been detected in some damned business or other, I suppose.

YORK   His correspondence has been broken open, in which he dwelt on the blessed hope of this country's returning to Rome.

CHARLES   S'blood, he's signed his own death warrant.

YORK   That is my fear, poor, faithful fellow —

CHARLES   (Starting up) James, you'll drive me mad! Poor faithful fellow indeed! Isn't it enough for you, that you flourish your religion to such an extent that you terrify the people into driving back every attempt at toleration I put forward! Aren't you content with making yourself so unpopular in your own person on account of your Popery that you've created a party who want to upset the order of succession? Isn't all this enough without you employing a secretary who gets himself indicted for high treason on the top of it?

YORK   Brother, I am most sincerely sorry...

CHARLES   Sorry! You'll be sorrier still before you're done. What is the use of my doing all I can to preserve the hereditary descent of the crown, secure that you shall come after me, when my every effort is negatived by your intolerable stubbornness and folly?

(YORK looks so miserable that the KING relents)

I was hasty, brother. We are as we are made, I suppose, but England at the present moment is like a cellar full of gunpowder, and you're going into it with a lighted match, to light a candle to your patron saint.

QUEEN   Is the danger so pressing, sir?

CHARLES   It is; there's a new sign of the times in London this moment. A scoundrel called Titus Oates says he's discovered a Roman Catholic Plot to kill the King. (Laughs) A Roman Catholic Plot! I've never had anything but kindness from Roman Catholics all my life, man for man, I'd trust their loyalty against the Puritans' any day, but this fellow has laid a deposition with one of the London magistrates, Sir Edmundbury Godfrey. However, Godfrey's a sensible man, and I'm in hopes the thing won't go any further. Otherwise it might ignite the whole of London.

YORK   Brother, I humbly beg your pardon for my neglect of your commands. I see that I am the cause of great trouble and inconvenience to you. If there were anything I could do…

CHARLES   Of course there's something you can do. (Persuasively) God knows I don't think the worse of you for being a Roman Catholic. But I do for the complete lack of common sense with which you vaunt the fact. If you mean to be a King, you must study something else besides your own private inclinations. Our mother's father was quite as sincere a Protestant as you are a Catholic; but he said, Paris is worth a mass. Can't you say, England is worth abstaining from a mass?

YORK   (With absolute sincerity) Brother, I am bound to obey you with my life, but even you cannot take my soul. My father died a martyr for his Church, and I will die a martyr for mine.

CHARLES   (Sitting down heavily and resting his arm on the table) Alas!

(Exit YORK)

QUEEN   Dear Charles, I am so sorry all this should have happened, they have been much to blame.

CHARLES   Thank you, Kate, let's turn to something cheerful.

QUEEN   Duchess, have you nothing to say to amuse His Majesty? (Her unspoken addition is: 'After all, it's what you're paid for.')

LOUISE   I protest, madame, I am so fluttered by what we have just heard, everything else has gone out of my head.

QUEEN   Pray tell His Majesty what happened at Lord Shaftesbury's; I daresay that will entertain him.

CHARLES   I hope it entertained the Duchess. I can't say that a dinner with Lord Shaftesbury is my notion of entertainment.

LOUISE   O sir, I was not thinking of myself! Lord Shaftesbury was so earnest in his invitation, that as I was telling Her Majesty, I thought I might as well go and perhaps establish friendly relations that might be to the good of all of us.

(Enter one of the QUEEN'S LADIES)

LADY   Your Majesty, pardon me, but has Your Majesty not heard?

QUEEN   What is the matter, Lady Roberts?

LADY   Your Majesty ordered your almoner to attend upon you at six o'clock?

QUEEN   Certainly. He is to tell me what I can give to His Majesty's hospital for the sailors.

LADY   But madam!

QUEEN   Well, what is it? It is time he was here, why doesn't he come?

LADY   Your Majesty...? (She looks at the KING)

CHARLES   Am I in the way, Lady Roberts?

LADY   O sir! is it possible Your Majesty hasn't heard?

QUEEN   (Impatiently) Heard what? Say what you mean, Lady Roberts. Where is Sheringham?

LADY   (In loud, desperate tones) In the Tower, madam, with four other members of Your Majesty's household; they were arrested an hour ago; the Lord Chancellor sent a body of men to take them up!

QUEEN   But what – why?

LADY   They are Catholics, madam, they say that something has been discovered which proves that all the Catholics in the kingdom are in league... (She wrings her hands and looks about as if she were going to faint)

CHARLES   Collect yourself, Lady Roberts, you must look after Her Majesty. She needs you. That's better.

QUEEN   (Faintly) Charles! It has come, what I told you of.

CHARLES   Nonsense, your servants shall be released immediately. Sheringham shall keep his appointment with you after supper. You must excuse me being an hour or two behind his time. As for the Lord Chancellor, I shall let him know that I intend to treat him more courteously than he has treated me, but I will inform him that I have taken them out again.

QUEEN   Dear Charles!

CHARLES   Did you hear anything else about the so-called Plot, Lady Roberts?

LADY   Only, sir, that it had all been made known to Sir

Edmundbury Godfrey…

LOUISE   Sir Edmundbury Godfrey, that was the name. Who is he, sir?

CHARLES   A London magistrate. A very well thought of man, he has friends in all parties.

LOUISE   But it was he Lord Shaftesbury has been speaking of today; he has been murdered.

CHARLES   What! Are you sure of this? When was it?

LOUISE   His body was found early this morning in Primrose Hill Fields.

CHARLES   Godslife! Have they no clue as to who did it? I should have thought he had no enemies.

LOUISE   Lord Shaftesbury did not say there was any clue; but was not he an enemy of the poor man?

CHARLES   Not that I know of; I know of no reason why he should have been: what makes you think so?

LOUISE   From the way his lordship spoke, he seemed so glad the body had been found dead.

CHARLES   Indeed! Had he any idea how it came there?

LOUISE   No, he had not, but he said that he dared say it would turn out that some Catholics were at the bottom of it…

QUEEN   (Gasping) Because of what had been told him about the Plot?

LADY   They wouldn't murder him. He's the most popular magistrate in London, it would cause the most fearful outbreak.

CHARLES   (As the realisation comes over him) Shaftesbury!
You devil!

C U R T A I N

SCENE IV

The King's drawing-room.

> (OATES is a singularly repulsive-looking man, who,
> however, conveys so overwhelming an impression of
> force that it is scarcely diminished by the manifest
> absurdity of his statements. Throughout the scene,
> SHAFTESBURY (facing audience) is smiling and
> sinisterly assured, guiding OATES through his worst
> blunders; the TWO (or other) LORDS cannot
> prevent themselves from being impressed by OATES;
> HALIFAX is angry with him, SUNDERLAND
> mocking, the KING both.)

1st LORD   Mr Oates, as Father Grove and Father Pickering
have been found guilty and executed on evidence brought by
you; and as my Lord Stafford also has been convicted in a trial at
which you were the chief witness, the matter is coming so near
the court, that His Majesty wants to have a first-hand account
from yourself of the Plot you have discovered.

SHAFTESBURY   Be so good, Dr Oates, as to relate the
particulars of the Plot for His Majesty's benefit.

OATES   Willingly, my lord, though I may mention, for the
profit of the Council in general, that I have already set forth my
findings in a printed work; some of the noble gentlemen may
have read it.

SUNDERLAND   (Bored, to CHARLES) I've seen a pamphlet,
sire, purporting to be by Mr Oates; it's about a hundred
and sixty pages long, it's called 'A short view of the Hellish
Discovery'.

CHARLES   Oh! Perhaps Mr Oates would let us have a still
shorter view?

SHAFTESBURY   The heads will be sufficient, Dr Oates.

CHARLES   The Lord Chancellor means the heads of the chapters, Mr Oates.

SHAFTESBURY   What are the aims of the plotters?

OATES   (Grimacing) The aims, my lord, are to overturn the Government, to disestablish the Church, (with fearful relish) to murder His sacred Majesty, whom they call (smacking his lips) the Black Bastard, and to set up the Duke of York as a Catholic sovereign in his place.

CHARLES   (Languidly) Comprehensive!

SUNDERLAND   No half-measures there, sir?

SHAFTESBURY   (Solemnly) And how did this information reach you, Dr Oates?

OATES   The Hand of God pointed before me. The outlines of the great Plot I gathered during my work abroad: the details I learned at home. The Jesuits now resident in the kingdom held a general consult on the 24th of April last, when they devised the details; I was present and heard them.

2nd LORD   It's true, Your Majesty, that the Jesuit fathers held their Triennial Congregation on that date.

HALIFAX   And where was this meeting?

OATES   At the White Horse Tavern.

CHARLES   At the White Horse Tavern. The Jesuit fathers meet at the White Horse Tavern!

SHAFTESBURY   If they had matters of this sort to discuss, sir, it is very likely they would choose an unusual meeting-place.

CHARLES   And how came Mr Oates among their numbers?

He is not a member of the order, I take it?

OATES   Heaven forbid, Your Majesty, that I should be mingled with their abominable foulnesses! But in the cause of God, I feigned myself to be one of them; I have lately returned from a sojourn in their college at St Omer.

SUNDERLAND   Is it true that you were expelled from the college for indecent practices?

OATES   (Sanctimoniously) Sir, Your Majesty, it pleased God to stir up their hearts against me, to revile and persecute me, but...

SHAFTESBURY   The innocent are frequently the victims of calumny.

CHARLES   (Pointedly) Very frequently, my lord.

SHAFTESBURY   With regard to the attempted murder of His Majesty...

OATES   (Greasily) Oh yes, the Jesuits as a body have sworn to carry it out; all over the world they have vowed to do it. In England, the Benedictines have offered a reward of six thousand pounds. In Spain, the college at Valladolid have promised ten thousand; in Italy, the Pope...

CHARLES   (Lightly) The Pope in league with the Jesuits to kill me! This is very astonishing, Mr Oates. His Holiness has frequently expressed condemnation of all extreme parties within the Catholic Church, the Jesuits among the foremost.

SUNDERLAND   Let him alone, sire. We shall have more presently.

SHAFTESBURY   Do we not often see, Your Majesty, that a common aim will override the minor differences, and combine enemies in the teeth of faction?

2nd LORD   (Eagerly) Who's to commit the murder?

OATES   Many have a commission to attempt it. Grove and Pickering, who have already been punished (glancing sideways at SUNDERLAND) on evidence it was in my power to bring; Mr Foggarty (leering) and the Queen's physician, Sir George Wakeman.

1st LORD   Weren't Grove and Pickering attached to Her Majesty's chapel?

OATES   O yes.

SHAFTESBURY   (Silkily) If anything less precious than His Majesty's person and the safety of the English Church were at stake, I should not do such violence to my own feelings as to pursue this enquiry farther.

CHARLES   (Cynically) I thank you, my lord.

SHAFTESBURY   Sir George Wakeman has of course been committed for trial, but the marshalling of evidence will in his case be a lengthy business. The outcome of the trial, touching the Queen so nearly as it does, will be of such extreme seriousness, that we are anxious to proceed with the utmost caution: and, I expect, were it not His Majesty's life that is concerned, I should be only too glad to turn a blind eye to Dr Oates's deposition on that matter.

2nd LORD   I cannot believe that Her Majesty could be remotely guilty of such a thing. Her devotion is so well known.

OATES   The wiles of the serpent, sir, are the undoing of many of the righteous. When your lordship has heard the evidence I have to bring against Sir George Wakeman, your eyes will be opened.

1st LORD   (Earnestly) It seems strange, Dr Oates, that all the members of this Plot should have taken you into their confidence?

SHAFTESBURY   It is the measure of Dr Oates's zeal, gentlemen.

2nd LORD   He <u>has</u> been wonderfully industrious.

(OATES looks at him benevolently)

HALIFAX   You point to four men, Mr Oates, who were actually entrusted with the task of butchering His Majesty.

OATES   (Malevolently) Those are all, my lord, whom I have been enabled to detect so far.

HALIFAX   Quite so, sir, quite so. You are, I believe, at present in receipt of fifty pounds a week, beside your board and lodging, which has been voted you by the House, in order that you may give your whole time to the service of the nation in unravelling the Plot. Naturally you would wish to keep this source of income open as long as possible; it might be inconvenient if you pledged yourself to make a final rounding up of the assassins.

2nd LORD   Indeed, my lord, Dr Oates has been very zealous: if what he says is true, he has saved us all from monstrous calamity…

SHAFTESBURY   (Calmly) Lord Sunderland, if you mean to charge Dr Oates with bearing false witness, that should be done at another time and place. At present, His Majesty wishes to hear Dr Oates's own version…

HALIFAX   Pardon me, sire.

CHARLES   Apart from the actual feat of murder, Mr Oates, the rest of the Plot was to be carried out by Lord Stafford, Lord

Petre and Lord Arundel?

OATES   Certainly, Your Majesty, Lord Stafford, as I have already been able to bear testimony, was, besides generally inciting and encouraging the other conspirators, to be the paymaster general to the Catholic army, those henchmen of the Whore of Babylon.

CHARLES   Yes, Mr Oates, at the time you originally made the statement implicating Lord Stafford, you said, if I remember rightly, that the commander-in-chief of the Catholic army, was to be my Lord Bellasis?

(OATES is silent)

You stated, in fact, that Lord Bellasis was to lead the troops in person?

2nd LORD   Yes, it's on record that he said that.

CHARLES   But while the charge against Lord Stafford was pursued, and has ended in his being sentenced for high treason, that against Lord Bellasis, who, according to your statement, was to take a much more prominent part in the rebellion, was dropped?

OATES   (After a pause) Yes.

CHARLES   Was that because you had meantime discovered that my Lord Bellasis is over seventy years of age and has not left his bed for the past eighteen months?

SUNDERLAND   Ha! Ha! Ha!

CHARLES   Really, Mr Oates, I feel that almost any other of the Catholic peers would have been a sounder speculation.

SUNDERLAND   Yes, sire, but Lord Bellasis was the obvious

choice for anybody who didn't know his lordship; on account
of his military record and his eminent position. Who among
the common people would fail to credit the authenticity of the
Popish Plot, when the Lord Lieutenant of the East Riding and
the Governor of Hull was implicated in it?

OATES   (Fiercely) My lord, if you make light of the
information I can bring...

SUNDERLAND   I shall live to see my entrails torn out and
burnt before my eyes by the public executioner, eh, Mr Oates?

SHAFTESBURY   Don't answer his lordship back, Mr Oates.
You are here for a weightier purpose. With regard to the charge
against Lord Bellasis to which Your Majesty has been pleased
to advert, I would beg leave to remind the Council that in so
widespread a conspiracy as this, many fish escape through the
net, do what we may. The charge may be wrongly preferred; that
does not say the substance of it is not correct.

1st LORD   Yes, there must be something there; witness
the evidence Mr Oates was able to bring against Grove and
Pickering and my Lord Stafford.

OATES   Is it not a sign to all men, my lord, that what I say
is the truth: that no sooner did I lay the information of this
hideous design with a magistrate, than that magistrate was
discovered foully done to death in Primrose Hill Fields?

SHAFTESBURY   There's a point, indeed, gentlemen. Who
killed Sir Edmundbury Godfrey, and why? Is not his death at
such a time and in such circumstances, the strongest proof of Dr
Oates's affirmations?

SUNDERLAND   So much so, my lord, that I suggest your
lordship should ask Mr Oates who killed him.

OATES   (Folding his hands, piously) You despitefully use me my lord; but my trust is in Him who hath cast down the mighty from their seats and hath exalted the humble and meek.

HALIFAX   I believe, Mr Oates, your chief trust is in the infatuation of the people, who are so mad with terror at the menace of a Catholic revolution that they'll swallow any...

(CHARLES gently lays his hand on HALIFAX's arm and the latter subsides)

CHARLES   It was during your residence abroad, Mr Oates, that you first got upon the track of this affair.

OATES   Yes, Your Majesty.

CHARLES   In the Jesuit College at Valladolid.

OATES   And in their college at Paris, Your Majesty.

CHARLES   And whereabouts is their college in Paris, Mr Oates?

OATES   Near the Louvre.

CHARLES   (Gently) You forget, Mr Oates, I also have resided abroad. The Jesuits haven't a college within five miles of the Louvre. You might as well say that Whitehall Palace is in Shoreditch.

SUNDERLAND   Ha, ha, ha!

1st LORD, 2nd LORD   How do you explain that, Mr Oates?

OATES   (Boldly) My lords, I have no more to say than this: what I know, I know.

HALIFAX   And what you don't know, Mr Oates, you invent.

SHAFTESBURY   Surely, my lord, one's recollection of a

foreign city is often much confused?

CHARLES   Well, perhaps Mr Oates retains a clearer impression of people than he does of places. You said in your original deposition, Mr Oates, that you were present at a secret meeting between the Grand Prior and the Cardinal Monsignore Vespucci. What sort of a man is the Cardinal to look at?

OATES   He is tall and dark.

CHARLES   Strange! When I knew him, he was short, but perhaps the Cardinal was a growing boy. And he had red hair. But perhaps he's dyed it.

2nd LORD   What say you to that, Mr Oates?

OATES   (Insolently) Gentlemen, either His Majesty or I must be mistaken. It does not become me to say more.

SUNDERLAND   I scarcely think it does, Mr Oates, unless you admit to the mistake yourself. You have been mistaken before now, have you not?

OATES   Sir?

SUNDERLAND   Yes, sir, when you were the curate of All Souls' Church at Hastings and you accused Mr William Parker of criminal practices, the jury found you guilty of libel and decreed damage of £1,000, did they not? And you were imprisoned in Dover gaol, and escaped from there to the continent.

OATES   The hand of the Lord delivered me out of the jaws of the ravening wolves.

SUNDERLAND   After your residence on the continent, in whatever capacity, you were, I believe, a chaplain in the navy? From which post you were expelled for committing the very practices you alleged to Mr William Parker?

CHARLES   Ha! Ha! Ha!

OATES   The Lord saw fit, for his own purpose, to suffer me to be thus calumniated by my enemies. But He has lifted me up out of the pit.

SUNDERLAND   And after that, Mr Oates, you obtained, how, you alone best know, the post of chaplain to the Protestant members of His Grace the Duke of Norfolk's household, from which you were expelled…

CHARLES   Oddsfish! Again!

OATES   I was, my lord, when the sons of darkness knew that I had obtained information of their vile designs they cast me forth; but it was the Lord's doing!

CHARLES   Your career, Mr Oates, seems to have kept the Lord very busy.

SUNDERLAND   O sire, the Lord began with Mr Oates long before that; he will tell you himself, that he was expelled from the Merchant Taylors' school, that he had to leave Caius College in a hurry…

OATES   (With a fierce snarl) My lord, I pray that God will soften your hard heart. I perceive in you, my lord, a great disposition to persecute the saints! Take heed, my lord, that you do not fall into the pit that is dug for the feet of the ungodly!

SUNDERLAND   I hope I have wit enough, Mr Oates, not to fall into any pit that is dug by you.

OATES   Sir, I have been the means of bringing a greater man than you to judgment.

HALIFAX   Do you threaten Lord Sunderland, you rascal?

OATES   I am in the hands of the Lord!

SHAFTESBURY   (Pacifically) Gentlemen, we stray from the point. We must not waste His Majesty's time. Dr Oates, pray give us, as concisely as possible, the facts of the evidence you have against Lord Stafford and Sir George Wakeman...

CHARLES   (Rising) I thank you, my lord. I have no wish to hear Mr Oates's evidence. Conduct Mr Oates elsewhere. Gentlemen, you may retire. I thank you for your attendance.

(The LORDS, with OATES, leave the room)

Lord Shaftesbury! Pray favour me with your attention for a moment.

(The OTHERS close the door, and SHAFTESBURY comes back, pale and smiling)

(Negligently) My lord, where was your humour, when you said the Catholics wanted to murder me?

SHAFTESBURY   (Smiling) In times of national crisis, sir, one has not the leisure for humour.

CHARLES   Strange. To my mind, one never wants it more than then.

SHAFTESBURY   (Drily) We are not all blessed with Your Majesty's volatile temperament. It is not everyone who can skate so merrily on the edge of disaster.

CHARLES   (Angrily) Disaster! You play on the people's ignorance and superstition till you get them mad with self-defence; then you can thank yourself for what disaster follows. You know as well as I do that this business is an impudent fraud...

SHAFTESBURY   (Coolly) I may know it, sir, but the people wouldn't believe it if they were told so by an angel from heaven. Their feeling has found vent in credulity over a Popish Plot; if this idea hadn't been to hand, they'd have found another.

CHARLES   That doesn't absolve you. You know that Stafford is innocent.

SHAFTESBURY   (With a smile and shrug) I regret the sacrifice, but speaking of that, would Your Majesty be good enough to sign the warrant for his lordship's execution? I have it with me.

> (He produces it from his portfolio. The KING takes it, looks at it, writes something on it, then signs it)

CHARLES   The sacrifice will not be quite of the nature you anticipate, Shaftesbury. I refuse to allow Stafford to be drawn and quartered. He will be beheaded. God help us, when that is all I can do for a man I know to be innocent.

SHAFTESBURY   The crowd won't like it, sir. It will be a great disappointment to them. After all, the sentence was passed on his lordship in a court of law.

CHARLES   Yes, and it is mitigated by the royal prerogative. Shaftesbury, why do you charge your soul with innocent blood?

SHAFTESBURY   (Coolly) Well, sir, we don't like the Duke of York. We don't want him, to put it plainly. Whatever I may think of the people's views, I am in agreement with them on that point, that a Catholic sovereign of so bigoted a temper, would be a national disaster of the first order. Your Majesty, left to yourself, would naturally not dispossess your own brother … so…

CHARLES   So I am to be refused supplies until I alter the succession?

SHAFTESBURY   It sounds ungracious, I'll admit, but that, I believe, is the scheme in a nutshell.

CHARLES   And because you know that the Parliament, left to itself, would not paralyse the Government, let the navy go to wrack and ruin and the home administration come to a standstill, you use this scare as a lever on them, and through them, on me...

SHAFTESBURY   (Bowing) Your Majesty chooses to put it so...

CHARLES   My lord, as Lord Chancellor – God save the mark – you have made a very honourable name for yourself by your honesty and zeal. Is it nothing to you that as one who has lately been celebrated as the honestest lawgiver alive, you stoop to bear false witness that would disgrace a vagabond thief? Lord Stafford is a man of blameless reputation. He has been very ill, he is so feeble he will have to be carried to the scaffold. The crowd that goes to see executions, my lord, is not the highest order of beings, but even with them, do you think that such a pitiful spectacle is likely to advance your cause?

SHAFTESBURY   (With masked eagerness) If Your Majesty is so much concerned for the pitifulness of the case, why do you not push the prerogative a stage further and grant his lordship a free pardon?

CHARLES   (Bitterly) Stafford has been found guilty by a jury of his peers; the trial was a loathsome farce, but apart from the activities of the arch-perjurer, it was within the law. If I pardon

[98]

Stafford, it won't alter the opinion of the public that he was justly condemned, and it will add fuel to the flames instead of water. To pardon Stafford means civil war. All this you know, Shaftesbury, and that is why you suggested my doing it.

SHAFTESBURY   (Laughing) Your Majesty was one too many for me there, I confess.

CHARLES   (Suddenly) Shaftesbury! What, in your opinion, brought my father to the block?

SHAFTESBURY   (Momentarily nonplussed) Why, sir, I presume it was a combination of unfortunate circumstances.

CHARLES   You are so staunch an admirer of Oliver Cromwell you ought to know that the deciding factor in the civil war was Cromwell's cavalry. And what, in your opinion, was the secret of that cavalry's success?

SHAFTESBURY   Well, sir, I don't claim to be a military man myself —

CHARLES   Nor do I, but as a boy of twelve in my father's camp, I learned a lesson I never forgot. The Royalist cavalry could make an excellent charge, and then it all went to pieces, and the effect of the charge was lost in waiting for the stragglers to come in. Cromwell's cavalry, my good Shaftesbury, was trained never to advance beyond a trot until the signal was given. They came on in one straight, unbroken line, and old Noll, riding ahead, could guide them with one movement of his arm, to whatever part of the field he wanted them to go. But do you know, Shaftesbury, I think that you are letting your cavalry get out of hand.

SHAFTESBURY   (Flippantly) I am obliged to Your Majesty for the hint.

CHARLES   There was a difference between my father and me, my lord. I am not the good man he was; but in a time of crisis – I do not – lose my head! Good morning.

> (The KING walks out, and SHAFTESBURY remains standing with his head on one side and his shoulder up like a vulture)

C U R T A I N

ACT III

SCENE I

The same – the King's drawing-room; evening.

> (The KING and NELL GWYN are sitting by the fire
> having supper at a small round table; a SERVANT
> is waiting on them and CHIFFINCH stands by in
> conversation with them)

NELL   (Resting her elbows on the table, knife and fork
pointing upwards) So you see, Mr Chiffinch, here we all are,
back from Newmarket a day before you expected us.

CHIFFINCH   Yes, indeed, madam; may I ask how the
accident occurred.

NELL   (Surprised) Haven't you heard about it from the King?

CHARLES   Faith, I was in such a hurry changing my clothes
to meet the Council, Mr Chiffinch and I have had no leisure for
gossiping.

NELL   It might have been disastrous. As it was, it was plaguey
unfor'nate. The house caught fire, and we were almost gutted in
our bed … (she corrects herself) beds.

> (The KING laughs)

CHIFFINCH   (Impassively) Most inconvenient, madam.
Thank God His Majesty was not hurt.

NELL   He was up in his shirt, ordering them all about; he had
the fire under in an hour.

CHARLES   I had had a little practice in the Fire of London.
Last night, thank goodness, we had no wind against us.

NELL   The house burnt down, none-the-less, so we just made
the most of what had been carried out; and back we came,

helter-skelter. It wasn't suitable to put up in the town, in the state we were all in.

CHIFFINCH   How did the conflagration start?

NELL   Lord, I don't know!

CHARLES   (Quietly) A groom was smoking his pipe in the yard too near a pile of hay.

CHIFFINCH   It has been a miraculous escape.

CHARLES   (Fingering the clock) Where is the Duke of Monmouth? He'll he glad to see his clock back again.

NELL   He'd better make haste or he'll find it all to bits! (She digs her elbow into the KING's ribs)

CHARLES   I shan't touch it, I assure you. (He opens the face)

CHIFFINCH   The truth is, sir, nobody knows where the Duke is. He rode off two days ago, very quietly, and no one has seen anything of him since.

NELL   I daresay he's mousing. And what's the news, Charles, since we've been away?

CHARLES   O, none to speak of; the trials go on, that's nineteen people executed over this damned business. And Mr Oates has presented the House of Commons with a bill for six hundred and eighty-seven pounds, twelve shillings and fourpence for expenses incurred in bringing the truth to light.

NELL   Save us! Have they paid it?

CHARLES   Indeed they have; I expect by now he's wishing he'd made it a round seven hundred.

CHIFFINCH   There was a good deal of feeling at Lord Stafford's execution, sire; that's the worst thing they've done so far.

CHARLES   My only hope is, that that scoundrel Oates having got so bloated with success, soon he'll contradict himself too wildly even for a jury terrified by a Catholic Plot.

CHIFFINCH   I am afraid there is a great deal of anti-Catholic feeling in the country, sir, irrespective of the Plot —

CHARLES   Of course there is; that's what the Plot-makers feed on.

NELL   Well, I'm no Papist; God bless Charlie and keep him long among us, is what I say.

(The KING kisses her hand)

But I don't believe the Catholics are trying to murder you.

CHARLES   Why should they? Nobody in their senses would murder me to put James on the throne.

CHIFFINCH   No, sir, but the people are terrified; that's what it is. They're all buying Foxe's Book of Martyrs and reading about what's going to happen to them when the Catholics set up the Inquisition. And Sir Edmundbury Godfrey's being murdered like that, as soon as Mr Oates had told him about the Plot, of course it looked very bad, madam.

CHARLES   Did you see anything of this procession on Wednesday?

CHIFFINCH   Yes sir, I went down and watched it. They had Sir Edmundbury Godfrey's effigy in front and a row of people dressed as monks with halters round their necks behind. And yesterday they took the horses out of Lord Shaftesbury's coach and pulled it up Cheapside, with all the mob yelling 'No Popery! No Slavery! Remember Sir Edmundbury Godfrey!'

CHARLES   Where was Lord Shaftesbury?

CHIFFINCH   In the coach, sir, grinning all over his face.

NELL   (Spitting on the floor) That's what I think of <u>him</u>!

CHIFFINCH   I quite agree with you, madam.

CHARLES   Chiffinch, I expect Lord Halifax to wait on me. When he comes, show him into my dressing-room.

CHIFFINCH   Very good, sire.

(Exit)

NELL   You know, Charlie, there's one good thing about this Popish Plot.

CHARLES   (Indulgently) Indeed! What's that?

NELL   You think twice before you take Portsmouth anywhere, and she daren't show her nose without you! (She laughs)

CHARLES   It's a very Christian spirit to find consolation in the workings of providence.

NELL   Charles, I hate that woman!

CHARLES   Well, my dear, I don't suppose she's particularly fond of <u>you</u>!

NELL   (Pleased) Ah, she's jealous of me, isn't she? It must be galling to her, when she's so grand and fine, and beautiful, too … she is beautiful, isn't she, Charles?

CHARLES   Very.

NELL   But all the same, she sees you throwing away your affections on a low-born, gutter-bred…

(The KING takes her into his lap)

CHARLES   Impudent…

NELL   Foul-mouthed…

CHARLES   Brazen…

NELL   Lewd…

CHARLES   Roystering…

NELL   Plain-faced…

CHARLES   Squinting…

NELL   Slut!…

(CHARLES kisses her)

NELL   But for all that, she might take a leaf out of my book.

CHARLES   How?

NELL   I never make a scene…

CHARLES   You don't – you little baggage? What about the time —

NELL   Unless I think it will amuse you. I don't know what occasion you were going to remember, but whatever it was, I am sure I only did it to please you.

CHARLES   I was thinking of the time you picked up the corners of the tablecloth, and launched the dishes into the hearth.

NELL   That might have happened to anybody.

CHARLES   Yes, it happened to me that time; me and my beautiful china dishes.

NELL   You didn't mind, did you?

CHARLES   O, not at all! But the Duchess, you know, has never thrown the dishes into the hearth.

NELL (Shrewdly) No, but she's often made you very tired and miserable, hasn't she?

CHARLES My dear, a gentleman can't say that ladies make him miserable, except by way of a compliment, you know.

NELL So much for high life; I shouldn't think it a compliment for a man to say I made him miserable.

CHARLES Come, Nelly; you must have made plenty of people miserable.

NELL Yes, but then I made them happy.

CHARLES Indeed, madam! I am sure you did.

NELL But I wouldn't now, Charles; I am as faithful to you as the highest-born whore you've got…

(CHARLES kisses her)

Do you know what I've had engraved on my warming-pan?

CHARLES What?

NELL 'I serve the King'!

(He kisses her and she gets up off his knee as someone is heard outside the closet door. CHIFFINCH enters.)

CHIFFINCH Lord Bruce begs a few moments with Your Majesty.

CHARLES (Gaily, standing up) Oh, come in, Bruce. Good evening. Well, you see me safe and sound. I expect the report alarmed you, eh? But there was no real danger in the fire, you know.

BRUCE (Speaking with difficulty) O sir! The fire! I bless God for it!

CHARLES Oddsfish! I can't say I go quite as far as that!

BRUCE   sire, I beg pardon. The Council has commanded me to inform Your Majesty, Your Majesty has escaped, by the blessing of God... (He shudders)

CHARLES   (Alert) What? What have I escaped?

BRUCE   Your Majesty returned to town a day earlier than was expected, and thus escaped an ambush...

CHARLES   What! Don't tell me this is some more of the Popish Plot, Bruce.

BRUCE   No, sir, no, no. Far worse, this is real! Six lords planned to seize Your Majesty as your coach passed the Rye House on the Newmarket Road.

CHARLES   Catholics?

BRUCE   No, sir, but as we think, though his name does not appear in it, under the guidance of Lord Shaftesbury. They meant...

CHARLES   (Grimly) I can guess well enough what they meant. Who were they?

BRUCE   A haywain was to be drawn across the road, Your Majesty, and when the coach drew up, musket men posted behind the hedges were to have fired upon Your Majesty and the Duke of York. Your Majesty's forced return threw them all into confusion, and the inferior plotters have confessed.

CHARLES   Who were the leaders? You spoke of six.

BRUCE   Lord Essex, sire; Lord Russell, Lord Howard of Escrick, Lord Grey, Sir Thomas Armstrong.

CHARLES   That's five; who was the sixth?

(BRUCE opens his mouth to speak, but says nothing)

(Kindly) If it is some friend of yours, Bruce, don't be afraid to tell me. I shan't love you any the less, and if I can, I'll help him for your sake.

BRUCE   (Hoarsely) Not for my sake!

CHARLES   Come! Who?

BRUCE   (After a moment) The Duke of Monmouth, sire.

(There is a long pause in which the KING seems turned to stone)

(Eagerly) He was led astray, sire. He had bad advice.

NELL   Charles!

CHARLES   (Dully) Where is he? Where's he gone?

BRUCE   He has left the other conspirators. It is thought…

CHARLES   Go! Send out after him! Bring him back! Why do you stand stock still? Do you want him to escape?

BRUCE   (Bravely) It's what you want, sir.

CHARLES   (Sitting down after a pause) Thank you, Bruce; you love me, don't you? You wouldn't have conspired against me, whatever advice you'd had.

BRUCE   O, God forbid, sir. If only I could do something —
(The KING makes a gesture with his hand)

CHARLES   But I doubt if he can escape, once this business gets abroad; he is so well-known! Is he to be brought back in chains?

(NELL comes forward and takes the KING's arm, looking up into his face)

NELL   Charles! For your own sake, you must do something for him.

CHARLES   (Bitterly) Are the others to suffer, and the parricide – the greatest scoundrel of the lot – to go scot-free?

(NELL lets fall his arm disconsolately)

(CHIFFINCH opens the closet door, beckons to BRUCE and whispers something to him)

BRUCE   (Gently) Lord Halifax attends Your Majesty's convenience.

(CHARLES slowly draws himself up and walks out through the closet door)

(BRUCE makes as if to speak to NELL GWYN, but she turns away and gives a sob)

(BRUCE goes out)

(The gallery door opens and MONMOUTH appears, white, exhausted, dishevelled and covered with mud)

MONMOUTH   Nell!

NELL   (Aghast) Good God! What are you doing here?

MONMOUTH   (Desperately) I <u>must</u> see him – I <u>must</u> <u>see</u> him, it's my only chance; if they find me before I see him, I'm as good as dead.

NELL   (Angrily) If you'd had your way, that's what he'd be now! He'd be lying in a ditch with his chest full of bullets, you brute beast…

MONMOUTH   (In despair) You don't understand, don't talk like that! I've got to see him. If they catch me before I see him, I'm a dead man…

NELL   You're anxious enough to save your own skin. You were quite cool, I daresay, when you were planning to murder <u>him</u>...

MONMOUTH   (Wringing his hands) Hush! Hush! Don't say it, Nell, help me, save me! (He seizes her hand and kisses it) You are so kind, so good! Help me! (He takes hold of her skirt and she pulls it away in disgust) Is he here?

NELL   Yes.

MONMOUTH   (Sounds off) O God! They'll find me before he comes!

NELL   Go over there.

> (MONMOUTH retires upstage and half-conceals himself in the window-curtains; after a moment's hesitation NELL goes and rings the bell. CHIFFINCH enters.)

CHIFFINCH   Yes, madam?

> (She hurries up to CHIFFINCH and as he catches sight of MONMOUTH over her shoulder and starts, she puts her hand on his breast pleadingly)

NELL   Hush, please! Don't call out.

CHIFFINCH   What is he doing here?

NELL   He says he must see the King...

CHIFFINCH   He can't!

NELL   O please! Please! He's repentant, look, he's quite worn out.

CHIFFINCH   This is impossible!

NELL   O, I beg you...

CHIFFINCH   (Wavering) Well…

NELL   Could you ask His Majesty please to come out?

CHIFFINCH   His Majesty is coming now, he'll be here in a moment, madam.

NELL   O thank God!

CHIFFINCH   (Takes a quick stride forward, and says to MONMOUTH) Turn out your pockets, sir.

MONMOUTH   (With a feeble attempt to swagger) How … how dare you?

CHIFFINCH   (Grimly) Turn out your pockets or I'll call the guard.

> (CHIFFINCH searches MONMOUTH and finds no weapon)

NELL   (Overcome by the indignity of the scene) O, Monmouth!

MONMOUTH   For God's sake, go away!

NELL   Yes, I will.

MONMOUTH   Thank you, Nell, thank you. Yes, leave me…

> (MONMOUTH retires up stage. CHARLES comes in, accompanied by HALIFAX)
>
> (Then exeunt NELL and CHIFFINCH)

CHARLES   The packet-boat will have arrived tomorrow if the wind doesn't change; the mails should be here by four o'clock. If they are, let the French Ambassador – (He sees MONMOUTH, gives an almost imperceptible start, and continues) tell the French Ambassador to come here immediately.

HALIFAX   Very good, sir.

CHARLES   I shall have the first half of my letter to King Louis written; I can't conclude it till I hear what instructions he has given to Monsieur Barillon.

HALIFAX   No, Your Majesty.

CHARLES   Let me see; the next session opens ten days from now; that gives me just time to get the matter arranged, provided no boats are held up in the Channel.

HALIFAX   Fortunately we seem to be having a very calm spell of weather for the time of year, sir.

CHARLES   Yes, I think I should like the Royal Society to give us a list of their readings and observations for the month; they can sometimes foretell a bad storm, and it is important to us to know as early as may be if one is likely to arise.

HALIFAX   I'll have an express sent down to Greenwich at once, sir.

CHARLES   Thanks, my lord.

HALIFAX   (With a meaningful glance) Your Majesty requires nothing more at present?

CHARLES   No, thank you.

(Exit HALIFAX)

(MONMOUTH comes uncertainly forward and stops. CHARLES takes up the clock, then puts it down again, and says suddenly:)

CHARLES   Why did you do it?

MONMOUTH   (Kneeling) O sir, I swear...

CHARLES   (Wearily) O get up, get up! (He walks over to the fire)

MONMOUTH   (getting ungracefully to his feet) I have come to ask your pardon…

CHARLES   For trying to take my life? Pray don't mention it.

MONMOUTH   I never meant to take your life…

CHARLES   It was to be done by somebody else, perhaps?

MONMOUTH   Not with my consent, I implore you to believe me. I joined this conspiracy, I wish I'd died before I'd done it, but I did it to safeguard you. I joined the enterprise because I knew that with me in their party, they would not dare to harm you…

CHARLES   What were the musket men doing behind the hedge?

MONMOUTH   They were to hold up the coach, to … to overcome the guard in case of resistance…

        (CHARLES is silent)

Don't you believe me?

CHARLES   No.

MONMOUTH   You <u>can't</u> believe I meant to take your life.

CHARLES   You were prepared to see somebody else do it.

MONMOUTH   It's not true! It's not true!

CHARLES   You were prepared to see me ride into an ambush of armed men (he raises his voice fiercely) who had their orders from Lord Shaftesbury. If you say you don't know what those orders were, you add folly to iniquity. I should be sorry to think a son of mine a fool as well as a knave.

MONMOUTH   (Throwing himself on his knees) Call me fool, knave, anything you like, but I am your son! O sir, can you think that all my affection for you has been a cheat?

CHARLES   (Raising him) If I did, I shouldn't despair; I don't lose any sleep over Lord Shaftesbury's trying to make away with me, but you – you who loved me – (pause) were prepared to... Well, that's how the world wags; I should have got the hang of it by now, but I confess you've shaken me a little. And tell me, I'm curious, what was to have been the proceeding after my death?

MONMOUTH   Don't speak that dreadful word. It was to have been an honourable captivity.

CHARLES   Oddsfish. That was kind, however; kind and thoughtful. And who was to have reigned during my honourable captivity?

(MONMOUTH hangs his head)

King Monmouth, eh? You poor simpleton: there would have been a usurper in my place, but he wouldn't have been you. And unless I'm greatly mistaken, King Shaftesbury would soon have found that my honourable captivity was a trouble and expense that any prudent man would do well to get rid of.

MONMOUTH   (Quite broken down) O sir, forgive me, forgive me! I know I don't deserve your pardon, but I ask it as your unworthy son; have mercy on me!

CHARLES   Ask your heart, Jamie, what end you really designed for me; did you mean to show me any mercy?

MONMOUTH   (Sobbing hysterically, flinging himself at CHARLES's feet and putting his arms round CHARLES's waist)

Dad! Dad! Don't let them put me in the Tower! Don't let them kill me!

> (CHARLES gently disengages MONMOUTH's arms and moves away from him. The latter gets up, looks at him eagerly.)

CHARLES   As regards your life – I pardon you that.

> (MONMOUTH seizes his hand and kisses it lavishly. CHARLES moves away as if he could not bear it.)

But you must go; I can't keep you publicly at court.

MONMOUTH   (Wildly) How can I escape?

CHARLES   I'll give you a safe conduct.

MONMOUTH   (With terrified cunning) You promise that?

CHARLES   (Coldly) I do. (He pulls the bell)

> (Enter CHIFFINCH)

Is Lord Bruce there?

CHIFFINCH   Yes, sire.

> (Enter BRUCE)

CHARLES   Lord Bruce, I want you to take the Duke of Monmouth to your apartments, and see that he leaves London at dawn tomorrow. A safe conduct will be prepared, you must give it to him and you may undertake to fulfil any requests of a private nature he makes to you, after his departure.

BRUCE   (Gently) Yes, Your Majesty.

CHARLES   Go quietly along the gallery and the Duke will follow you; stop if you see a crowd of people. Get him to your rooms as secretly as you can.

BRUCE   Yes, sire.

> (He goes to the door and walks out of it, cautiously)

> (MONMOUTH, left alone with CHARLES, turns round and stares at him with a frightened, stupefied look)

CHARLES   (Gently) Now follow Lord Bruce.

> (MONMOUTH runs softly to the door like an escaping animal; then he turns round)

MONMOUTH   (Hoarsely) ... Good-bye?

CHARLES   (Carelessly) O, good-bye. (He rings the bell)

> (Enter CHIFFINCH)

> (MONMOUTH steals out)

Chiffinch, I should like some brandy.

> (CHIFFINCH opens the cabinet and brings out a decanter and glass. He pours out a glassful and hands it to the KING, who stands drinking it with his back to the fire. As he does so a small procession as for evening prayers – TWO CHORISTERS with tapers, TWO with Bible, etc., FOUR LADIES-IN-WAITING on the QUEEN – come, from the gallery entrance and pass across the room to the closet; everyone makes an obeisance to the KING in passing; it is plain from their faces and the QUEEN's especially, that they know of the tragedy. The last to come is the BISHOP with his Bible in his hand.)

Good evening, Dr Ken. I am afraid I shall not have the benefit of your ministrations this evening.

KEN   (Simply) God be with Your Majesty, wherever you are.

CHARLES   (In a bitter, satirical manner) Dr Ken, you have very often reproved me for my loose life…

KEN   I did what I conceived to be the duty of my office, sire.

CHARLES   (Mollified) And you have always done it in a very gentlemanly manner…

    (KEN bows)

You now have a prime illustration ready to your hand; my son, sir, conceived in lust and brought forth in shame, has attempted to do away with me. There you have a text for as fine a homily as was ever preached; (savagely) but pray don't make use of it!

KEN   (Kindly) Your Majesty, if it were my duty to speak boldly in times past, it is no less my duty to speak comfort now.

CHARLES   Comfort!

KEN   As a priest, I charge you to seek it where alone you may find it. As a man, I would say I am heartily sorry for Your Majesty.

CHARLES   Thank you, Ken.

KEN   I thank God Your Majesty escaped unhurt! There are to be public thanksgivings in the churches.

CHARLES   (Absently) He looked so white!

KEN   (Firmly) Don't let your mind dwell on him, sir.

CHARLES   You haven't any children, have you, Ken?

KEN   No, but I would remind Your Majesty of a great King who suffered as you do, and yet God was with him.

    (CHARLES is looking into the fire; seeing that he is

not listening, KEN opens his Bible and reads)

And behold, Cushi came, and Cushi said: Tidings, my lord the King, for the Lord hath avenged thee this day of all them that rose up against thee. And the King said unto Cushi, is the young man Absalom safe? And Cushi answered: The enemies of my lord the King, and all that rise against thee to do thee hurt, be as that young man is. And the King was much moved, and he went up to the chamber over the gate and wept; and as he went, thus he said: O my son Absalom, my son, my son, Absalom! would God I had died for thee, O Absalom, my son, my son!

(KEN closes the book and walks quietly into the closet)

(The KING sits down by the fire and buries his face in his hands. As he does so, the clock strikes eight.)

SCENE II

The King's drawing-room. A very dark day outside spreading a
general cheerlessness over the scene.

(The QUEEN stands by the table talking to
CHIFFINCH)

CHIFFINCH   His Majesty will be with Your Majesty
immediately.

QUEEN   Thank you, Mr Chiffinch. Are all the trunks packed
for Oxford?

CHIFFINCH   Pretty nearly, madame. His Majesty must make
a very early start, you know.

QUEEN   Yes: that is why I wanted to be sure of seeing him
this evening.

CHIFFINCH   Won't Your Majesty please to be seated?

QUEEN   Yes. (She sits down) What is the use of their going
down to Oxford to open Parliament —

CHIFFINCH   (Surprised) But, madame! The London
streets are filled with rioters – they might besiege the House of
Commons —

QUEEN   Oh yes! I know, I know what the streets are like, Mr
Chiffinch, because I and my people have been asked not to show
ourselves in them. (With bitter vehemence) But what is the use
of running to Oxford when we must carry Lord Shaftesbury on
our back?

(CHIFFINCH sighs)

Titus Oates is very strong now, isn't he, Mr Chiffinch?

CHIFFINCH   I'm afraid so, madame.

QUEEN   Quite like an ogre in a fairy tale.

CHIFFINCH   (Violently) Worse!

QUEEN   (Simply) You know, Mr Chiffinch, I am very sorry for people who have no faith in God; because when things become very bad, as they are now, how do they bear it?

(CHIFFINCH kisses her hand)

(CHARLES comes in L. and CHIFFINCH goes out with a bow)

(The KING looks sad and ill, but his demeanour is negligent and quiet)

QUEEN   (Rising) Charles, I would not worry you. I have something to say that I hope will give you pleasure.

CHARLES   (Gently) What is that, my dear?

QUEEN   The Parliament's order that I should keep only nine Catholic ladies.

CHARLES   Yes?

QUEEN   I have thought it best not to show any favouritism, so I have arranged that my ladies shall ballot for the places —

CHARLES   (Absently) Yes?

QUEEN   (Shyly) Except the ninth, dear Charles. I have allotted that place already. To the Duchess of Portsmouth.

(The KING looks at her, only half comprehending)

(Taking his hand) At a time like this, you must have everyone about you who can give you joy or comfort.

CHARLES   (Impulsively) No one gives me more comfort than you. Thank you, my dear. Your kindness means more to me than your kind act.

QUEEN   (Standing with her head on his shoulder) I want to say to you, once and for all: I know I am the next victim of the Plot. The day after tomorrow you must meet Lord Shaftesbury's Parliament, is it not? They will get rid of poor James first, then me.

(He is about to speak)

Hush! Let me say this, Charles, it is my last chance, before – who knows what! I know you won't let them kill me but if – when, they demand my divorce – banishment – you must do what is best. Don't throw away any advantage for the sake of keeping me. Let me show you that I love you, by making you promise —

CHARLES   Catherine!

(A sound as of a hurried approach is heard outside the gallery door. The DUCHESS OF PORTSMOUTH enters in a distracted state)

LOUISE   Sir – Your Majesties – Sir, you must protect me – what can I do – you must save me?

CHARLES   What is the matter? Of course I shall protect you.

QUEEN   (Kindly) Take courage, Duchess, you are quite safe in His Majesty's protection.

LOUISE   (Frantically) We are all undone, madame. They say that the first demand Parliament will make will be that all Catholics shall be banished from the court. You and I, madame, shall be put into the Tower. We shall probably be executed without trial. My God! Why did I ever leave my home? (She cries hysterically)

QUEEN   (Soothingly) Now, now, Duchess. This is being foolish. Leave her to me, Charles. You are distressing His Majesty, madame. He has so much to bear! Now, calm yourself, there's a good creature.

LOUISE   (More coherently) O madame! The tales are so dreadful. If anybody speaks in favour of us, Titus Oates says: You're a Papist! I'll remember you for it! And the next thing they know is they are accused of being in the Plot! Is there no hope for us?

CHARLES   Your best hope – the best hope for all of us – is in courage like Her Majesty's. But you may be certain, your life is perfectly safe.

LOUISE   O I hope so, I hope so! What have I ever done to be cast away in this barbarous country?

QUEEN   Come, Duchess, you'll be more comfortable in your own apartments, your maids will look after you; I should lie down, for a little —

LOUISE   I'm going to pack!

        (She rushes out, leaving the gallery door open)

        (The QUEEN laughs gaily)

QUEEN   I too will say good-bye, dear Charles.

CHARLES   (Rapidly, with intense seriousness) Do you know what I have been remembering all day?

QUEEN   (Eagerly) No?

CHARLES   When I was escaping from this country, I was on the coast with the soldiers coming nearer and nearer to my back, and no tide – no tide to carry me out to safety. But I knew if I stayed where I was, the tide would turn.

(She looks at him silently; he kisses her hand and leads
her to the door, then comes back and stands looking
into the fire. Without any warning, SHAFTESBURY
appears at the gallery door, looks into the room and
comes in. He has dispensed with any ceremony and his
behaviour is one of insolent triumph.)

CHARLES   (Looking up with displeased surprise) You
dispense with ceremony, my lord!

SHAFTESBURY   Your Majesty has always appeared to dislike
ceremony. Certainly in private life it is an encumbrance.

CHARLES   But who is talking of private life?

SHAFTESBURY   (Rubbing his hands) O, no one, sir – at
present.

CHARLES   (Between his teeth) What do you want, my lord?

SHAFTESBURY   I think it is only right to warn Your Majesty,
the temper of both Houses is such that when you meet them
the day after tomorrow, they will not vote one penny until Your
Majesty gives your consent to a bill excluding the Duke of York
from the succession.

CHARLES   Indeed!

SHAFTESBURY   You see, sir, there is no other means, in their
opinion, to avert the danger of a Catholic tyrant. There is no
possibility of another heir to Your Majesty. If Your Majesty had
been a little more complaisant to the claims of the Duke of —
(He stops, feeling that even he has gone too far)

CHARLES   Who is to succeed me?

SHAFTESBURY   There is some talk of course, of offering the crown to Your Majesty's nephew, the Prince of Orange; but for my own part —

SHAFTESBURY   You had rather not. William of Orange would be backed by Dutch money and a Dutch army, and your ambition of a republic would be further off than before.

SHAFTESBURY   Your Majesty is correct, as ever. No, we feel, my friends and I, that it does not really matter very much, which course Your Majesty adopts. Sign the Exclusion Bill, and acknowledge your defeat, resigning your powers into our hands: or refuse it, and when the present Government has collapsed for want of money, my friends and I will form a government. So far as we are concerned, the absence of an heir is not of very great importance.

CHARLES   Quite the contrary, I perceive.

SHAFTESBURY   But out of consideration for Your Majesty, I would suggest that signing the bill would be a more dignified and comfortable method of capitulation, than waiting to be starved out.

CHARLES   You may be right, my lord, in thinking that Kings are a bad invention; but while they remain in being they must do their office. It is my duty to see that the descent of the crown entrusted to me is not tampered with for private advantage, I must see that my brother or his children succeed me. What happens when I am dead, is not my concern, I shall offer to Parliament when we meet on Thursday, either that the Duke of York shall become King in name only and rule by a Regent: or that one of his daughters shall be my heir.

SHAFTESBURY   And I am empowered to tell you, sir,

that Parliament will refuse your offer without an instant's deliberation.

CHARLES   (Slowly) Parliament is you and your friends. If I dissolved Parliament, I would not be afraid to face my people – my people, who come to see me feed my ducks, and run after my coach, and back my horses at Newmarket.

SHAFTESBURY   No doubt, sir. But it is not the horse copers and idlers who supply Your Majesty with cash. You may make what retrenchments you please in your amusements, but without the sums voted by Parliament, your government is ruined; and I think that even Your Majesty must know it.

CHARLES   You wouldn't risk all this without the people's consent, Shaftesbury. Are you sure you have it?

SHAFTESBURY   If I may merely take the liberty of reminding Your Majesty that we are all removing to Oxford by Your Majesty's express desire, because the people of London are so wild in their support of me and my party – I scarcely think there is any point in prolonging this interview. I will wish Your Majesty good evening and good-bye, till we meet at Oxford!

> (He gives a cackling laugh and goes out)

> (CHARLES instantly darts across and pulls the bell. Enter CHIFFINCH)

CHARLES   Light the candles.

> (CHIFFINCH lights a branched candelabra on the table. It is now heavy dusk.)

Now call two of the guard and post them outside that door. Wait! Then find Monsieur Barillon; give him the cloak and hat and bring him in the private way as quick as possible.

(CHIFFINCH hastens out. CHARLES sits down at the table, and takes writing materials from the drawer; he begins to write out a statement.)

(In a few seconds the arrival of the GUARD is heard outside the door. In another moment, from L., the FRENCH AMBASSADOR enters, fantastically enveloped in a big cloak and hat which he at once takes off.)

CHARLES   Ah, Monsieur Barillon. I am sorry to have made you assume such an inelegant disguise, but it is of the utmost importance to me that no one knows anything about this interview. The guard are posted outside that door. Mr Chiffinch keeps the other.

FRENCH AMBASSADOR   (Panting) Don't mention it, Your Majesty.

CHARLES   Now, we have no time to lose. Not an instant for policy or politeness. The moment has arrived, Monsieur, when I am being forced to exclude the Duke of York from the succession, and the natural step for me and my Parliament to take will be to offer the crown to my nephew the Prince of Orange.

FRENCH AMBASSADOR   But sire – no, no, it must not be —

CHARLES   (Relentlessly) He will have all the Low Countries amenable to his influence and the resources of England into the bargain —

FRENCH AMBASSADOR   Such a piece of treachery to His Majesty the King of France – it is unthought of!

CHARLES   O no it isn't, Monsieur! Two such clever people as the King of France and you must have thought of it very often, and decided what you'd do if the emergency arose, now – here it is. How much are you empowered to offer me?

FRENCH AMBASSADOR   Mon Dieu, sire —

CHARLES   We'll take all that as said, Monsieur. Come; how much?

FRENCH AMBASSADOR   B-b-but —

CHARLES   Are you good for six hundred thousand pounds?

FRENCH AMBASSADOR   Sacre bleu! No, no, no, impossible.

CHARLES   Five hundred thousand? You must remember that a war against Holland and England would cost you three times as much.

FRENCH AMBASSADOR   (Groaning) Oh! Oh! Oh!

CHARLES   (Sternly) Four hundred thousand, Mr Barillon, and that is my last word. I am not going to hold out for the succession unless I have the means of doing it. I shall agree to the Parliament's proposal and write my nephew a cordial invitation —

FRENCH AMBASSADOR   No, no! Yes, yes, yes. sire, yes, we will pay that.

CHARLES   Are you empowered to sign for His Majesty?

       (BARILLON nods)

There's the pen.

       (He puts it into BARILLON's hand, who signs.

CHARLES sands the paper, and puts it into his breast pocket.)

FRENCH AMBASSADOR We can't pay it all at once, sire.

CHARLES Of course not, over a period of two years will do, and remember what I shall be forced into doing if I don't get it!

(BARILLON totters out, L.)

CHARLES Chiffinch! Dismiss the guard! (Aloud, to himself) Good-bye, my lord, till we meet at Oxford!

SCENE III

The Geometry School which has been temporarily converted to the House of Lords. Centre back, a small dais with a state chair and half-concealed by it a small, nailed trunk. At right angles to the dais, two rows of benches facing each other. The scene is so arranged that what is seen appears to be the top of a large room.

Two college servants are straightening the carpet on the dais and giving a last sweep up.

1st S.   Oxford's never been so full since it was raised.

2nd S.   What with the Parliament and the lords and gentry and the court there isn't room to sneeze. The nobility are crammin' on top of one another. I hear Mr Pettigrew has got two lords in each bedroom and three honourables in the attic.

1st S.   Ah, but <u>somebody's</u> got room to move! You 'ear Lord Shaftsbury's got the whole of Balliol to himself and his servant.

2nd S.   Not quite to himself. Dr Oates is with him.

1st S.   Come to see the results of his handiwork?

2nd S.   Why? There's not to be any executions, is there?

1st S.   Lord, man I mean the whole of <u>this</u>. Why does Parliament meet at Oxford instead of in London? Because the Popish Plot has put everybody beside themselves, and those London men are asking for a chance to set to and break each other's heads. That's all Dr Oates's work where it isn't Lord Shaftesbury's. I've always said the people of London was a huneducated lot.

2nd S.   Ah. They ain't scholars, that's where it is. But Lord Shaftesbury's got the King in a cleft stick. Do you hear that his lordship plans to take command of the militia the moment that Parliament has refused all supplies?

1st S.   Refused... <u>all</u> supplies?

2nd S.   Not a penny piece is His Majesty to have till he's sworn that Lord Shaftesbury shall have his say in everything.

1st S.   Well, he's not the man for my money, I can tell you. I don't like him. I've seen his paces and I don't fancy him.

2nd S.   Maybe you don't, Zacchary Wilberforce, maybe you don't. I don't say you aren't right, though I've known you many times when you was wrong. You'll recollect of how you would lay five shillings on French Lady and make me do the same, though my mind misgave me all the time, and sure enough, she wasn't so much as placed —

1st S.   Have it your own way, Jonathan, have it your own way. We all knows that when you wins it's your own doing, and when you loses it, it's somebody else's. But speaking for myself, I'd take a wager now that His Majesty will have a trick up his sleeve even now...

2nd S.   So, no, not now. I wish he had. But it stands to reason he can't do nothing now. And whatever he does can't make no difference in the long run. They'll say to him: Sign the Exclusion Bill and out the Duke of York, then we'll see whom Lord Shaftsbury has got ready to put in his place —

1st S.   And we won't have to look far either —

2nd S.   O don't sign it, then we refuses the money and you can shut up shop.

1st S.   Talk of shutting up, what's this here box?

2nd S.   It was brought in by one of His Majesty's gentlemen.

Put there special. I reckon it's something His Majesty don't want to lose sight of. If you ask me, it's some ready cash and a few clean shirts.

1st S.   Do you mean he's going to bolt?

2nd S.   Never you mind what I mean or what I don't mean. All I says is, His Majesty has had some experience of travelling and he knows it's inconvenient to be separated from his luggage.

1st S.   Lord bless us!

2nd S.   Mind you, I'm sorry. I've always been one to speak a good word for His Majesty. He's an easy man and a proper spoken sort of man, and the sort of man I likes to see about, which is more than I'll say for somebody else but he's no match for <u>him</u>, more's the pity.

1st S.   I'm not so sure. I wouldn't bet on Lord Shaftesbury 'til I see him at the winning post.

2nd S.   Ho, and you wouldn't believe but that French Lady would be an easy winner, though. I told you at the time…

1st S.   All right, all right, all right, I said I done wrong there, didn't I? But I'm a man that likes a bit of a flutter, and I don't mind laying you three to one that His Majesty will have a little surprise for somebody before he's finished.

2nd S.   It's taking your money, but I reckon you owe me something for that bet on French Lady.

> (Exeunt. SHAFTESBURY, accompanied by TITUS OATES and a LORD, enters L.)

OATES   The great and terrible day of the Lord is at hand.

SHAFTESBURY   It is. And my friends will find that I don't forget them.

LORD   Your lordship has not disclosed what form the constitution is to take. I don't want to pry further than my neighbours but I hope that I may have some opportunity of continuing to devote my services to your lordship.

OATES   In such an overturning of the powers of darkness and establishing of the reign of truth, your lordship will have particular need of men about you whom your lordship can trust.

LORD   This is not a moment when one thinks of self, but some small appointment, not too far from the centre of affairs.

OATES   All we wish is an opportunity to devote ourselves to the service of our country.

> (During this conversation the hall has been gradually filling with gentlemen who take their seats, either on the right benches as the KING's supporters or on the left as SHAFTESBURY's men)

SHAFTESBURY   Of course, of course, naturally. my dear friends, your support has been everything to me. Where should I be without it in the future? As for places, so many will become vacant in an hour or two's time, I shall find no difficulty in rewarding my friends even to the top of their deserts.

OATES   I hope that your lordship won't allow the man Charles Stuart too much rope. Why should we be kept out of our own while he makes up his mind to the inevitable?

SHAFTESBURY   Oh, not too much, Dr Oates. Just enough rope to…

> (He pauses delicately)

LORD   The Queen will of course be banished?

SHAFTESBURY   Yes, I think something of the kind can be

come to. I should be sorry to cause her any unnecessary hardship or inconvenience, but I really think she will be more comfortable elsewhere.

LORD   And the King?

(At this point CHARLES followed by BRUCE enters quietly and makes for the dais. As he takes his seat, the gentlemen rise and sit down again. SHAFTESBURY then takes his seat amid clapping from his side of the benches. He gets up and bows regally to his supporters. Indignation is indicated among the KING's benches but they also express resignation and hopelessness. SHAFTESBURY rises again and addresses the King without ceremony.)

SHAFTESBURY   I hope Your Majesty is prepared for the events which the coming session must bring forth?

CHARLES   I hope so, my lord.

SHAFTESBURY   If it is not too late to advise Your Majesty, I should suggest that you don't prevaricate or play with the assembly. Parliament is in no temper to be played with, sir.

CHARLES   I daresay not.

SHAFTESBURY   Naturally I shall do my best to shield Your Majesty from any awkward consequences of your folly and misdemeanours..

(A voice from the KING's benches cries out)

VOICE   For shame, my lord!

(The KING makes a slight motion with his hand to check it)

CHARLES   You are very good.

SHAFTESBURY   But even I can't undertake to protect you beyond a certain point. Parliament is absolute master now, sir, and anyone who does not realise that has a very uncomfortable time ahead of him.

CHARLES   No doubt, sir.

SHAFTESBURY   And Parliament, I say again, will not be trifled with.

CHARLES   Indeed, my lord, nothing is farther from my thoughts.

(OATES and four of SHAFTESBURY's supporters make the following interruptions:)

OATES   He hath cast down the mighty from their seats and hath exalted the humble and meek.

1st   No Popery, no slavery!

2nd   No support for toleration of the Catholics!

3rd   No money, sir, for alliance with the French!

4th   No money, no money, not a sixpence, not a sixpence!

OATES   He filleth the hungry with good things but the rich He hath sent empty away.

1st   No Popery!

2nd   Remember your father, sir, we are in no mood to have our wills crossed by you.

3rd   Remember your father!

OATES   Your Majesty was pleased to be very harsh with me

when I testified before Your Majesty, very harsh and scornful to me. It was a pity, it was a great pity that Your Majesty's ears were stopped against the truth. A stiff-necked generation, a race of sinners, I fear. Your Majesty will be driven out to be a by-word and a shaking of the head among the nations...

SHAFTESBURY   Gentlemen, silence, I entreat. Your Majesty, it is our wish that everything should be done seemly and in order. I have no doubt that Your Majesty is prepared to submit to the inevitable with a good grace. You have been called the father of your people...

CHARLES   I have, I believe it has sometimes been objected that I am the father of too many of them...

OATES   Sinfulness and abomination...

SHAFTESBURY   Will nothing teach you, sir? Your jests will do you no service here. They fall on deaf ears here, I promise you.

1st   An end to this tomfoolery.

2nd   Sign the Exclusion Bill!

3rd   Sign or you starve!

SHAFTESBURY   Sign or you starve. Your answer to that, sir!

ALL   Your answer! Your answer to that, sir! Your answer!

> (CHARLES rises to his feet. BRUCE, unnoticed, has opened the box behind him and stands ready for a sign from the King.)

CHARLES   My lords and gentlemen, my answer. The realm has been much disturbed of late by many problems, and the parties and passions arising from them have brought us to the verge of the most horrible catastrophe with which a people can be visited. I mean a civil war. As we can by no means be brought to one mind, and as our strife is driving the nation to a calamity which it is my duty as the sovereign to avert by any means within my power, therefore I have thought fit to put an end to your debate.

> (CHARLES holds out his arms and BRUCE swiftly puts the robe over his shoulders and hands him the crown which the King puts on his head)

And I now declare both Houses to be dissolved.

> (For a moment there is complete silence and the gentlemen retain the positions they held a moment ago, as if they were frozen. Then one lord from SHAFTESBURY's benches breaks noisily away and runs out, and his exit starts a panic. CHARLES's supporters crowd round him but do not mount the dais so that his head is still visible above them. As SHAFTESBURY's men hurriedly make their way out, he, showing greatness in not being overwhelmed, tries, but in vain, to hold a handful of them together.)

SHAFTESBURY   Gentlemen! You curs, do you show your tails?

1st   The game's up, my lord!

> (Exit)

SHAFTESBURY   My lord, stand fast and save what you can…

2nd   It's enough for us if we can save our skins.

> (Exit)

4th   It's France. Did you never think of that?

SHAFTESBURY   Yes, but I did not think he had the time.

(Exit 4th lord. A 5th approaches SHAFTESBURY.)

5th   My lord, my lord, make haste!

(A burst of cheering from outside)

It is dangerous to stay, the tide has turned.

SHAFTESBURY   He was waiting for the tide, but I thought he'd starve first.

(More cheering)

5th   What's to be done, my lord?

SHAFTESBURY   Tell them to bring the coach to the next corner. If we aren't away in half an hour, we shall be here till tomorrow morning.

(More cheering)

There goes my republic! The fools. But I gave them a run for their money. I shan't be forgotten.

(Exit SHAFTESBURY. CHARLES's LORDS speak partly among themselves, partly to the KING.)

1st Lord   Sirs, I can't believe that ten minutes ago we were all shaking in our shoes.

2nd   Lord Shaftesbury has travelled a good way in ten minutes: from the top of the tree quite to the bottom.

3rd   God damn me if I ever saw such a crew. If this is Shaftesbury's House of Peers, I thought, his Cabinet will be like something out of Newgate or Bedlam.

1st   As His Majesty was not to be a King anymore, they saw no reason why they should be gentlemen.

2nd   The roads will be in fine confusion.

3rd   Thank God we don't need to fly, I shouldn't care to make my escape through such a mob as that.

2nd   How will Your Majesty return?

CHARLES   Quite easily, I believe.

BRUCE   His Majesty anticipated some slight congestion of the route. The Life Guards are keeping open the first mile of the London Road, and the postillions have been in the saddle for the last half hour. It will take the coach about three minutes to wheel off, I fancy.

1st   Again, our joyful thanks…

2nd   God's blessing on Your Majesty.

3rd   We will retire and wait upon Your Majesty in London.

2nd   Should there be any hostile demonstrations, we will stand between them and Your Majesty with our lives.

CHARLES   I thank you heartily gentlemen, but I do not expect any hostile demonstrations.

1st   Where is Lord Shaftesbury?

CHARLES   I should imagine that Lord Shaftesbury is making for the continent. If only he had waited, I could have given him some excellent addresses.

3rd   We'll wish him a good voyage and Your Majesty a comfortable journey back to town.

        (EXEUNT the LORDS)

CHARLES   Oh, help me off, Bruce!

(BRUCE takes off the robe and folds it over his arm.
The KING takes off the crown and holds it)

Half an hour ago you had many masters, now you have one.

BRUCE   The only one I'll ever own, sire. Oh it was
magnificent!

CHARLES   Yes, I'm afraid, Bruce, it's been something of a
blow to them.

BRUCE   It's annihilation, sir.

CHARLES   I have done my best for my brother. What he will
do, God knows. But I have done my best to preserve the lawful
descent of my crown.

BRUCE   I have two messages, sir, which I was asked to deliver,
but I had no opportunity.

CHARLES   What are they?

BRUCE   Her Majesty the Queen said that she would follow
you all day in her prayers.

And Mistress Nell Gwyn sent you her love.

(The King smiles but says nothing)

BRUCE   Shall I take the crown, sire?

CHARLES   No, Bruce. I think I can carry the crown.

C U R T A I N

Baliol Holloway as Richard III.

An extract from

The View From Downshire Hill: A Memoir
by Elizabeth Jenkins

During my first, enchanted, visit to Stratford, the company was led by Baliol Holloway and Dorothy Green. They were both highly successful at Stratford, where Ba was, for years, the centre of an enthusiastic cult. They never quite gained star status on the West End stage, though throughout the Twenties Ba was idolised at the Old Vic; his tall, broad-shouldered but gaunt figure, his inimitable voice which reminded you of the echo of waves sweeping into a cavern, were not suited to the sophisticated light social comedy of the era. He was, however, very successful in the Shakespeare seasons in the Regent's Park Open Air Theatre (which he described as 'half-salary and double pneumonia'). Someone who brought a Russian friend to the Regent's Park production of *As You Like It*, in which he played Jacques, said that the Russian had declared that he had never seen, and had never expected to see, on the English stage, anything like such an impression of philosophy and melancholy.

Most actors, I suppose, are very good raconteurs. Ba was. He was extremely fond of Gilbert and Sullivan's operettas, and he told me that once, as a schoolboy, he had made his mother give him the money for a seat at a Savoy matinee – I think it was *The Yeoman of the Guard*. He said Sullivan himself was conducting with a white flower in his buttonhole. Before the overture his score slipped off the stand and several members of the orchestra stooped to grab it. Ba also told a story which I do not think is in print. Gilbert was telling Sullivan his idea for the story of *Iolanthe*. He said: 'The young man is half a fairy.' Sullivan said: 'Which half?' Gilbert, furious at being interrupted, exclaimed: 'What does it matter, which half?' Sullivan said: 'I should think it matters to Iolanthe.'

In the years immediately before the war, Ba had a very good season under the management of Sydney Carroll, who leased the Ambassadors' Theatre, small and very conveniently sited just off Leicester Square. Here Ba produced *The Rivals*, in which he played Sir Anthony Absolute and Lady Tree played Mrs Malaprop. After this he produced Wycherley's *The Country Wife*, in which he played Mr Horner. This obscene and delightful comedy had a most successful run. He produced and acted in these seventeenth- and eighteenth-century comedies with a sense of period that was positively illuminated by his physical presence. As Charles Lamb said of William Smith's performance of Charles Surface: 'he took the eye with a certain gaiety of appearance.'

But none of this was enough of what he wanted. The gnawing misery of an actor who has a following and a well-founded confidence in his own powers, but sees the steadily ebbing tide, 'by chance or nature's changing course untrimmed', the long pangs of disappointment, the suffering of what is felt as a continual, undeserved rejection, are dreadful to experience, even at second hand. Ba had always said he wanted a play about King Charles II. Arthur Bryant had succeeded with one about Pepys, *And So To Bed*, in which Charles had an important part but not the lead, and there was room for another. I undertook, under Ba's supervision, to write one. The chief interest in the one we projected was the episode between the King and his favourite bastard, whom he had created Duke of Monmouth, and who betrayed him – seduced by Lord Shaftesbury into a plot to assassinate the King, after which Monmouth himself would reign as Shaftesbury's puppet. The discovery resulted in the hurried banishment of Monmouth to save him from execution for high treason.

It was extremely interesting to me to work with someone so steeped in theatrical experience. Sometimes, when I thought a scene had reached its climax, Ba would produce a further one. Very interesting, too, was that when he felt the dialogue should be a little longer at a certain point in the scene, he hadn't the words but he would beat time for as long as the few extra lines would last. He got the play put on at the Theatre Royal at Windsor for a week, with himself in the lead. I was thrilled by every minute of it. It had such packed houses that when Lyn Harris, the headmaster of St Christopher's at Letchworth, where I had had most of my education, tried to get a seat on the last night (which I am sure I could have got for him if I had known he wanted to come) he was told they were sold out.

Anyone who has had a play considered for the West End will know all of this story – the highly distinguished names who almost accepted it, the times success was almost in the bag and then evaporated. One near miss was an approach from Ivor Novello. He was still at the height of his theatrical success, but told me that the time was coming when he wouldn't be able to sing and dance any more, and he wanted a full-scale romantic part in which he could graduate into a serious phase. He had seen the play at Windsor and he said that if I'd given the chief part to Monmouth instead of to Charles II, he would have bought it as it stood. He asked me if I could rewrite it, to arrange that? I said yes, and rewrote the script, enlarging Monmouth's part by the inclusion of Lady Henrietta Wentworth, with whom Monmouth had a passionate love-affair. Ba of course helped me with all this, and we hoped that Novello would cast him as Charles II. The final disappointment was acute, but even then I could see how interesting it was from the professional point of view. Ivor Novello said, after reading it: 'I can't do it, I'm too old, I could come on and hold it up for ten minutes, and after that, no one would believe a word I said.'

There was, however, a treat in store: under the title *King Monmouth*, which was what the wretched young man allowed the mob to call him, the BBC made a gripping radio version of it. Ba was an acclaimed Charles II, supported by an excellent cast, and the music from Purcell's *Dido and Aeneas* emphasised the emotion. Ba and I were listening to it in the little glass box in the studio. Norman Wright was then one of the BBC Directors of Drama. This was the first time I had met him, but later I had the delight of a friendship with him and the actor Robert Harris. When Norman heard that I was in the listener's box, he came to speak to me; he said it had made him weep: 'I cried over it.' The production was so successful they repeated it twice.

The View From Downshire Hill by Elizabeth Jenkins, published by Michael Russell (Publishing) Ltd, 2004.

A note on the text

YORK makes the following speech in Act I: 'The last time that the assassins permitted him to see his children, he said to me that the rebels might try, in the absence of my brother, to make one of us younger ones a puppet in their foul designs, and he charged me that I must never allow myself to be made King while my brother lived. I replied: "I will be torn in pieces first." I was nine years old at the time, and I have been told that my reply struck the bystanders as something remarkable.'

It was Henry Duke of Gloucester, not James Duke of York, who in fact delivered this reply.

MARGARET ELIZABETH JENKINS OBE (31 October 1905–5 September 2010) was an English novelist, playwright and biographer of Jane Austen, Henry Fielding, Lady Caroline Lamb, Joseph Lister and Elizabeth I.

She went up to Newnham College, Cambridge in 1921 to read English and history, though women were not eligible to receive a degree from the university until 1948.

Her 1934 novel *Harriet*, a fictionalised account of the Harriet Staunton affair, starved to death for her inheritance, won the Prix Femina.

The Tortoise and the Hare (1954) is regarded as Jenkins's most successful novel. Hilary Mantel commented that Jenkins 'seems to know a good deal about how women think and how their lives are arranged'.

In 2004 she published a memoir, *The View from Downshire Hill*. Jenkins died at the age of 104 in 2010.

Printed in Great Britain
by Amazon

26906398R00091